Contents

A selection of the general interview questions and answers
featured in this book is available to download and print out
from the Kogan Page website.

To access simply go to
www.koganpage.com/SuccessfulInterviewSkills
and enter the password: SI5719

Successful
interview skills

How to prepare, answer tough questions and get your ideal job

5th edition

Rebecca Corfield

913 000 00101390

London and Philadelphia

To TB

First published in 1992
Second edition 1999
Third edition 2002
Fourth edition 2006
Fifth edition 2009
Reprinted 2009

Kogan Page Limited
120 Pentonville Road
London N1 9JN
United Kingdom
www.koganpage.com

Kogan Page US
525 South 4th Street, #241
Philadelphia PA 19147
USA

British Library Cataloguing in Publication Data

A CIP record for this book is available from the British Library.
ISBN   978 0 7494 5652 8

Library of Congress Congress Cataloging-in-Publication Data
Corfield, Rebecca.
  Successful interview skills : how to prepare, answer tough questions and get your ideal job / Rebecca Corfield.--5th ed.
       p. cm
  Includes index.
  ISBN 978-0-7494-5652-8
  1. Interviewing--Handbooks, manuals, etc. 2. Self-presentation. I. Title
  BF637.I5T44 2009
  650.14'4--dc22   2009012312

Typeset by Saxon Graphics Ltd, Derby
Printed and bound in India by Replika Press Pvt Ltd

Introduction

The importance of interviews

Imagine you have been applying for jobs recently. Today an invitation to an interview arrives. How do you feel as you read the letter? Elated, inspired and raring to go? Or terrified, resigned to your fate and overcome with a sense of impending doom? Does this second description sound like the way you would be feeling? Feeling down about your chances, writing off your skills and experience and convincing yourself that you won't get anywhere? Perhaps that is the way that you have reacted to being called to interviews in the past. There is nothing more likely to make that gloomy prediction come true than mentally closing down your chances of success right from the outset.

You should feel excited and enthusiastic if you get the chance of an interview. Wasn't this why you applied for the post in the first place? After all, you went for the job because you wanted a chance to prove to the employer that you would be the best person for the job. You put in all the effort needed during the application process because you wanted to be awarded the position. It is very rare to receive a job offer without having a job interview first, so getting an interview brings you closer to your desired goal. However, you are not alone in feeling dread at the thought of having to put yourself on show before a potential employer. We all share the worry that we will not come across well when under scrutiny, and we all fear that we will go through the stress and strain of getting prepared for nothing as we will not be in with any real chance of getting the job anyway.

Negative attitudes such as this represent the kiss of death for any job interview. If you start out feeling unconfident there is a danger that you will enter the interview itself labelling yourself a loser. A negative attitude will be noticed by interviewers immediately. They are alert to candidates who are uncomfortable and ill-at-ease, and are less likely to be impressed by them than those who appear more relaxed and sure of themselves. If you really want to move jobs, get promoted, change your career and get ahead, isn't it time you found out how to take more control when putting yourself forward? The familiar patterns from the past of worry and failure can be changed. You do not have to keep on falling into the same traps that you have been setting for yourself. Turning natural worries and fears into determination and dynamism is the subject of this book, and it can teach you how to make these changes in your own life.

Interviews are a fact of modern working life and the skills needed to do well at an interview will be used by us all many times throughout our lives. Most jobs are filled using these one-to-one meetings between the employer and the best applicants, but interviews are needed in a variety of other situations too. Whether applying for a job, a promotion, a training programme, a college course, or even a bank loan, we all need to know exactly what is involved in the process of interviews, and about how to impress people at first meeting and in a short space of time. With part-time and temporary work increasing we will all be attending interviews more frequently from now on and the sort of interviews we have will be varied. You may be talking to a recruitment agency, be called in to see an employer for an informal pre-interview discussion, or be interviewed for a job over the telephone or via the internet.

The skills involved in creating a favourable impression on others and presenting ourselves at the interview are the same set of skills that make us confident at meeting people in any situation – whether at work or socially. If you know how to generate a positive effect, how to have an impact on others and present yourself as an interesting and valuable person, you will be a winner in all areas of your life, not just in the interview room. Your self-confidence will grow, your social poise will be enhanced in a variety of situations such as making new friends, having discussions with potential business partners or funders with regard to setting up your own business, or talking to clients and customers once you are in a job.

Interviews are difficult and a strain at the best of times and there are few people who really look forward to the experience. Even the most confident and extrovert of candidates will suffer from the jitters prior to walking in to the interview room. Whether applying for a course or a job, appearing in front of just one person or a panel, you need to know how to present yourself confidently and enthusiastically. Interviews are often seen as the one big hurdle between us and the job we want. We feel we are in control of what we choose to include in our CV or on the application form, but the interview seems much more unpredictable and uncertain. However, an interview, whether for a job vacancy or any other purpose, is really a marvellous opportunity. Why? Because you are in control of the way you come across during the interview. The way that you choose to act and sound and the answers that you decide to give, all contribute to forming the impression that the interviewer will be left with.

Many people think that it is a pure fluke whether they are successful in interviews or not. To them, the outcome seems to depend on whether their face fits, being in the right place at the right time or some other unidentifiable cause. But the outcome of the interview process is *not* merely determined by chance. We are able to exercise considerable control and influence over the way the interview is conducted and, more importantly, over the outcome.

You, for instance, will decide how to dress and act and exactly what you want to convey about yourself. Your history, experience and skills are not just a list on a sheet of paper; they represent the story of your life which needs to be explained and shown in a positive light. No one can talk for you in the interview room – that is part of the reason that it is a daunting prospect, but it also enables you to be in charge of the way you come across to the other people present. No one can *make* you look or behave in a way that you do not want to. In the same way you cannot be made to say anything you do not agree with. Let us hold on to this comforting thought. Although it may be difficult to believe when the offer of an interview arrives, the interview will go the way that you lead it. Of course you will not be in control of selecting the panel of interviewers and it is not up to you to choose the candidates also going for the job, but all the aspects of your own behaviour on the day are in your control. There are many things that you can do to improve your chances of appearing to be the best person for the job on the day.

Needless to say, attaining this level of control involves some effort. You will have to do some initial work on yourself to get this to happen. First you will need to do some planning work to think about your strengths and weaknesses; how others see you; what your work history conveys to other people; what impression you want to create when you walk in to the interview room and how to correct any incorrect judgements that may be made about you. Secondly you will need to do some preparation. You will need to think about how you will answer interview questions and particularly which aspects of your working life you want to bring to the fore and which you want to leave in the shadows; you will need to concentrate on your body language and facial expressions and you will need to work on controlling your nerves under pressure.

How to get the most out of this book

This book can show you how to begin to exercise more control over interviews. Whether you are applying for jobs or courses at the moment, learning about interview techniques for the first time, advising other people on the best way to approach interviews, or if you just want to refresh your techniques for the future, this book will be able to help. For no matter how many times any of us face the interviewer across the table, we can still learn how to refine and improve our performance and put ourselves across more positively. You may have picked up this book just to reassure yourself that you have not forgotten anything, especially if it has been a while since you last attended an interview. You may feel worried that you may not come across well when the time comes to meet potential employers.

Some of the advice given may seem to be common sense but, when running training courses in interviewing skills and personal presentation, I am often surprised to find that such basic points need re-stating, and that is why they are included here.

Of course, I do not claim that this book will make you successful at getting *any* job, and I assume that you will only be applying for those vacancies for which you can reasonably expect to be considered. However, if we study the candidates who are successful at interview, we will discover some common characteristics which are listed later on in this book.

Chapter 1 describes the interview process, explaining exactly what happens in an interview. Looking specifically at job interviews, we consider what employers are trying to achieve by using interviews as a method of selecting staff.

Different types of interview are covered so that you know what to expect in a variety of circumstances. Chapter 2 moves on to look at the whole interview process through the eyes of the employer. It covers the 10 most common mistakes that people make and also gives the recipe for success in interviews. Chapter 3 introduces planning for your interview and preparing for the big day. Suggestions include ways of finding out more about the employer; considering all aspects of the job; thinking through the image you want to portray and how to anticipate all the important aspects of the interview in advance.

Chapter 4 describes how to create the best first impression that you can. It covers what makes up the image that we convey in an interview, focusing on body language, personal appearance, using your voice and controlling nerves. In Chapter 5 the nerve-racking task of giving a presentation as part of your interview is explored. This chapter looks at how your presentation should be put together and outlines methods of generating extra impact with the audience.

Chapter 6 moves on to give 50 sample questions that are likely to crop up at your interview. Suggested answers are included across the whole range of questions, together with advice about how to handle especially tricky situations that may occur. In conclusion, Chapter 7 draws all this information together and provides a step-by-step guide to successful interview skills.

At the end of each chapter you will find handy lists of what to do and what not to do, which summarise the key aspects in the text, together with some specific points to remember as you move forward. Details of some helpful internet resources are given in Appendix 1 at the end of the book. You will find everything you need in this book to increase your chances of succeeding at your next job interview.

The interview

What is an interview?

The dictionary defines an interview as a face-to-face meeting for the purposes of consultation. In other words, it is a discussion between two or more people for one reason or another. Organisations, companies and institutions use this method of meeting and discussion to help them choose the best candidates to employ.

By far the biggest cost to an employer is the staff or workforce. Wages and salaries often make up 70 per cent or more of a business' total costs and the price of advertising for new staff is high. Apart from being expensive, making mistakes in recruitment can cause major problems. As well as being awful for the person concerned, a worker who is unhappy or unable to do their job properly can be a great burden, and if conflicts develop they could destabilise the whole team and may ultimately jeopardise the output or function of the entire organisation. Obviously decisions about who to employ have to be taken very seriously.

It is therefore not surprising that employers spend a great deal of time and money trying to ensure that they pick the right person for each job. In this context, the right person means the individual who will contribute most to the good of the company or organisation and who will repay the time and money invested in them as an employee by staying with the company and performing well.

Types of interview

Interviews come in many shapes and sizes depending on their function. Most interviews are for the purpose of selecting someone for a job vacancy. The employer, senior managers or human resources (often abbreviated to HR) staff will meet with possible candidates, ask them a series of questions and then decide which person to offer the job to. Not all interviews are to do with applying for jobs though. For example, you may be interviewed to become a college student or to secure a place on a training course, to start voluntary work or to join a social club or society. Starting a new job does not necessarily mean that you have done your last interview for a while either. Many of us will be frequently interviewed once we are in a job, or studying on a course, by our supervisors, managers or tutors. These interviews can have a variety of purposes: to appraise or review our progress; to monitor our performance in the job; to consider specific projects; to help us plan our future development; to resolve work or study problems and sometimes for mediation or disciplinary matters if work difficulties persist.

Your ability to perform at these kinds of interviews once in a job can be a significant factor in your future career development. Your profile with your managers and your reputation in the organisation can be affected by the way you handle all your interview experiences. Every event from regular work or team reviews to personal development planning and performance appraisals is a form of interview and needs your effective participation to make it a success. What these different types of interview have in common is the need for you to put yourself across clearly, by showing your unique contribution to the team effort as well as your individual skills and strengths. You need to know how to plan ahead for every type of interview, how to prepare adequately for them all and come over at your best from start to finish.

About interviews

The people who interview you for a job are likely to be complete strangers, unless you are applying for a vacancy in an organisation in which you already work. Most of us would prefer to face people we do not know at interview as this makes it easier to describe ourselves freely, putting the slant we want on our answers. However, not all panels are composed of unfamiliar faces. Finding ex- or present employers on the interview panel can be disconcerting and it can feel constraining when trying to describe our best behaviour when members of the panel may have had experience of us at our worst!

When you are invited for an interview, it will usually take place in a private space where your discussion will not be interrupted or overheard. The exact physical arrangements will vary according to the kind of job you are applying for. Interviews normally take place sitting down and can range from an informal chat in easy chairs over a coffee table to a formal panel interview (ie with more than one person interviewing) across a leather-topped boardroom table. More junior jobs tend to be decided by a one-to-one interview, usually with the employer, line manager or direct supervisor for the post in question.

Panel interviews

Panel interviews, where more than one person conducts the interview, are usually held for more senior roles or where responsibility for overseeing the vacancy is divided between different people. An example could be for the post of a customer care manager. The Director of the organisation may be present together with the Head of Customer Relations and the Human Resources Manager. In larger organisations a member of the human resources department will often be present to ensure consistent standards of interviewing are maintained for the recruitment of all staff and to provide specialist employment information and advice, if needed.

Other assessment methods

Interviews for jobs with larger companies or for more senior roles are sometimes part of a much more complicated and extended selection procedure that can involve exercises, discussions, group activities, presentations and tests. These activities are designed to assess how the personality and values of the candidate fit those of the organisation and to test their intellect and ability. Often the exercises used are based on potential workplace situations. These simulations are intended to be more objective than just using an interview as they allow candidates to show their behaviour in a live situation rather than just talking about examples from their past. They also allow candidates to be assessed over a wide variety of tasks rather than just at an interview.

Sometimes these selection procedures take place at what is called an assessment centre, often based at the head office of the organisation concerned, although it can also be at a hotel. The title, 'assessment centre', conjures up a picture of a specialised venue just for assessing candidates, but this is rarely the case. It just refers to the range of assessment activities that have been decided upon for a particular selection and the venue is the one that is most convenient for the organisation. You will normally be given an outline of the kind of activities that you will face before the interview, which can give you the chance to prepare as much as possible for them. However, often the exact detail of the particular exercises will remain a secret until the day you attend the centre.

Tests can range from written papers to assess your personality, aptitude or abilities, to informal social groupings to assess your 'fit' into the group of staff with whom you would be working. Case studies, role-play, negotiation exercises and team challenges can all be used.

Tests will be used to check your technical or specialist understanding of problems. Some aptitude tests look at general abilities or your capacity to thrive in particular employment positions. General management vacancies may use this kind of psychometric test to see if you are suited to high pressure group leadership. Some employers such as the Armed Forces also put candidates through a series of physical challenges such as an obstacle course to test fitness, determination and initiative. In-tray exercises for jobs that involve strategic decisions will ask candidates to work against the clock to analyse and prioritise a file of paperwork, some of which conflict so that you are forced to make choices about where your priorities would lie.

You may, quite often, also be asked to give a presentation on some aspect of the position applied for, as part of the selection process. If this is the case it will be made clear in your letter of invitation to the interview. Chapter 5 covers in detail how to handle giving such a presentation.

Why do interviews take place?

Interviews are held to gather information and to appraise character. In an interview for a job the employer first selects those applicants who seem worth interviewing. The next step is to find out which of the shortlisted candidates (those chosen for interview) would be the most suitable person for the job.

If I asked you to find out about somebody whom you had never met before, you would probably choose to talk to that person face to face. Interviews are just a common-sense way for people to meet, find out about each other and ask each other questions. So, as well as the employer seeing you, you also have the chance to make your own decisions about the employer, the job on offer and the type of organisation or company concerned.

If you are selected to come for an interview there is every chance that you could end up getting the job. The employer likes what you have said about yourself so far and wants to know more about you.

What happens in an interview?

After applying for a job, you will be informed that the employer wishes you to attend at a specific place and time and you will probably be one of a group of people who have been shortlisted or specially chosen, from all the others who also applied for the position, to be seen individually by the employer. The employer will have sifted through the applications for the post, selecting for the shortlist those who best fit the specification for the job and those whose details on paper seem to represent having some kind of extra value to them.

You will be asked to confirm that you are able to attend the interview. On the day of your interview when you arrive at the company, if you have not already completed an application form, you may be asked to complete a form giving your personal details. At the appointed time you will be called in to the interview room and invited to sit facing your interviewer, often across, or around, a table or desk.

The employer will ask you questions for a period of between 20 minutes and an hour on average, depending on the type of job applied for and the level of your experience and qualifications. Interviews for more senior jobs can take longer. At the end of this time you may be able to ask the employer some questions relating to the position applied for. (Chapter 6 contains more information about the type of questions that you may want to ask at this point.) This normally marks the end of the interview.

It is quite common for the interviewer to take notes about your answers in order to remember the main points after your discussion so do not be rattled by this – just ignore it. For some jobs you will be asked to prepare a presentation on your ideas for the position. If so, this usually takes place before your interview begins. It can be a valuable chance to put across ideas you think can contribute to the organisation. Chapter 5 tells you how to approach this task.

What are interviews about?

Interviews are like examinations at the end of a course of study. You know that you have done well so far on the course, and you know in advance roughly what areas the questions are going to cover. In the same way you know that you have done well in the selection process up to this point, or the employer would not have invited you for the interview. You also know in advance roughly what will be covered in the questions to be asked. This often surprises people but most interviews are very similar in their content and the majority of questions you will be asked are predictable. The sample questions in Chapter 6 cover most that you will ever be faced with in a job interview

What leads to success in interviews?

In the same way as thorough preparation leads to success in examinations, so a system for approaching interviews can have the same outcome. Most of the talking done in the interview will be by you. This means that you can have a fair measure of control in deciding where the interview is going. You cannot set all the questions yourself, but you can calculate fairly accurately what subject areas will be covered and plan your answers accordingly.

Of course, not every interview you attend will be successful and even the most successful careerist will fail many interviews, but still end up in rewarding and challenging work. The best approach is to try to present yourself in the best way and treat each new interview as a learning experience.

Dos and don'ts

✔ Do be prepared to do some work in advance to help you do your best.

✔ Do treat each interview as a chance to see what you think and feel about the employer.

✔ Do approach each interview positively – it may be an opportunity to move your career forward.

✘ Don't turn down an interview just because you are scared – this job could have your name on it.

✘ Don't think that you can just breeze in – proper preparation is vital.

✘ Don't let panic get the better of you – you are more likely to succeed if you keep calm.

Points to remember

1. Keep an open mind about what you may be faced with in the interview. More varied methods of selection are now being introduced.

2. Try not to live in the past. Just because you were not successful in previous interviews does not mean that the next time will be the same.

3. Avoid trying to fake your answers in tests. Most tests are sophisticated enough to spot any inconsistencies in what you say.

4. Be yourself: if you are not successful it may be that a better job for you is just around the corner.

5. Almost everyone who was ever employed had to go through a job interview to get where they are today.

2

What employers are looking for

The only reason why you will be invited to an interview is because the employer wants to find out more about you to ascertain whether you are the best candidate for the job. Sometimes people believe that they are called in to be tested with trick questions or put under pressure. This is very rarely the case. No sensible employer can afford the time for, or the expense of, such games. You will be interviewed for one purpose only – to find out exactly who you are and how you would deal with certain situations likely to crop up in the job.

You are only there because your initial approach, whether through application form or curriculum vitae (CV), has interested the employer enough to want to know more. Whatever you have said so far has worked.

Case study

A business, Stephens' Circuits, needed a new supervisor for their main depot. They had an internal candidate who had been taking on the role temporarily for the last six months and they thought he would be ideal for the job.

However, they wanted to be fair in their recruitment practices so they placed an advert in the local press and Jobcentre Plus. Four people were shortlisted from the 20 who applied.

On the day of the interviews, one of the external candidates so far outshone the favoured internal candidate that she was unanimously chosen for the post. Her preparation for the interview, her knowledge of the work and her enthusiasm for the role won her the job. The internal candidate, however, felt embarrassed at having to sell himself in front of familiar colleagues, answered in monosyllables and did not give any evidence that he would be the best candidate.

Even when your chances are limited in relation to other candidates, if you perform best on the day of the interview, you may win through to get the job, even when another candidate looks more promising on paper.

Providing proof that you are the right candidate

If you have been called for an interview, there is no reason why you should not be the person who eventually gets offered the job. You stand just as much chance of being successful as any of the other candidates to be interviewed. How you have positioned yourself so far has worked. The way you described yourself on the paper application has appealed to the employer and you are amongst the front runners to get the job. To capitalise on your success so far, you must research thoroughly exactly what you put in your CV or application form. The mixture of your background and your current situation has appealed to the person short-listing for the interview.

Let us consider the interview situation for a moment. What is happening there? A strange situation has been set up – we do not normally have to talk to total strangers about our personal details but in a job interview we have to divulge everything about our background, experiences and personality to the employer. This situation arises because the employer has something that we want – the job – and we are 'on show' to convince them that we are the most suitable candidate for that job. The best candidate on the day may not be the one with the longest experience or the widest set of skills, as this could be ascertained from a simple comparison of the application forms. It will be the person who seems to fit in best and is most impressive on the day of the interview and this is why your whole performance will be taken into account when the decision about who to give the job to is made.

Employers have to make their decision based on three areas relevant to any job:

■ your qualifications and skills – what you know and what you can do;

■ your experience and work background – where you have been and what you have done;

■ your personality and character – who you are and how you behave.

The most important of these is the last one. Candidates may fall short of the advertised skills and qualifications for a job and often too lack the required experience but still manage to convince the employer that they are the best candidate on offer. How? By stressing that they have the right personality to fit into the organisation and contribute fully to the fortunes of that company. Skills can be taught and experience can be gained once in the job if necessary – but one's personality cannot be changed so easily.

In a competitive job market where there may be many competent candidates for every job, satisfying these three bullet points (page 19) are the minimum required for possible employment. Where several able and experienced candidates are in front of an interview panel they will make their decision based on two more factors:

■ your vision – your ideas about how you see the job/department/organisation developing;

■ your added value – that extra something that you can contribute over and above the other candidates.

Most employers are not experts on the job that is covered by the vacancy. They are busy each day running the organisation or the department and they need to employ someone who can come in and do the job as advertised. Ideally the person recruited will hit the ground running once in the job, ie be able to start working effectively right from the first day. They will be clear about the priorities and certain of the best way to move forward. The employer will be able just to hand over the reins and leave it all up to the new employee to make it all work properly.

This is where the bullet point above about having some vision comes in. You need to really think about the job, imagine yourself doing it and then look ahead to envisage:

■ What will be involved – what will you be doing when you begin work?

■ What three key things do you think it will be most important to do when you start?

■ Where do you think this job is going in the longer term?

If you can convey a sense that you can 'own' this job and look after the part of the business it concerns, you will come over as a very valuable addition to the organisation. No employer wants a new person at work who has to have their hand held for the first three months of their employment. This would be just too much of a drain and a responsibility, and represents a major investment of time and trouble. Employers want you to be able to come in, settle in and get stuck in straight away with the minimum of fuss and effort.

The most common mistakes

In my research with employers over many years, these are the 10 most common reasons for failure at interview.

1. Arriving at the interview unprepared for what is to follow.

2. Having a sloppy appearance or too relaxed an attitude to the interview.

3. Not showing any excitement about, or enthusiasm for, the work.

4. Not seeming to understand the requirements of the job properly.

5. Not showing that they have fully considered all aspects of the vacancy, eg indicating a dislike of paperwork when it is clear that this will form a large part of the job on offer.

6. Not answering the questions fully and giving answers that are too short.

7. Being vague about details and just providing lots of unstructured waffle in their answers.

8. Not being clear about their skills and abilities, ie being too vague or modest.

9. Seeming overly concerned with what they can get from the job rather than conveying exactly what they are offering.

10. Using pretentious language or jargon instead of normal speech.

Do any of these numbered points look familiar to you? Most people have been guilty of one or more of them during interviews. Normally it is feelings of nerves that stop us from coming across at our best. We fail to hear the questions properly; lose the thread of what we are trying to say; totally forget the excellent examples that we prepared to talk about and feel embarrassed about blowing our own trumpet too much.

It is obvious that this type of behaviour is not going to help anyone get a job. However, it is useful to realise how interviews are lost so that we make sure we are aware of what *not* to do. Then we can concentrate on acting in a way that will ensure that we are successful.

Reasons for success

These are the 10 qualities that are most in demand by employers:

1. Flexibility.

2. Helpful and caring attitude to clients and customers.

3. Supportive team member.

4. Keen to take on responsibility to organise people or projects.

5. Having a positive attitude in the face of difficulties or challenges.

6. Displaying enthusiasm for the work.

7. Able to handle change.

8. Looking smart.

9. Ready to participate in continual learning.

10. Good time-keeping.

Jeremy, an employer from a large international company, said to me, 'passion and optimism are very infectious.' This applies just as much to the private sector as it does to the not-for-profit sector. Obviously if you are applying for a job with a campaigning charity, you will be expected to understand what the organisation is campaigning for and demonstrate commitment to this cause. But private sector employers will also want you to be motivated by the way they operate and to be excited by the goods and services they sell. For these businesses, quality can always be improved, more effective sales techniques can be developed and customer care enhanced.

De-mystifying the interview

Employers are often bad at interviewing people. Have you ever had an interview where the employer did all the talking, or where he just did not manage to put you at ease at all, or where she arrived late and seemed confused about the exact job applied for? This sort of thing can happen when the interviewer is either not competent, not trained or not prepared for the occasion. Many people who are roped in to conduct interviews have had little or no formal training in this subject. Even if they have, it takes the right kind of personality to be good at interviewing other people and to bring out interviewees' good points. It may surprise you to know that most interviewers are fearful when conducting interviews and display high levels of anxiety about the task.

However, defects in an interviewer's technique need not matter too much, although it can be helpful to be forewarned about such a possibility. Ultimately, it is up to you to prepare yourself so well that the interviewer's shortcomings will not distract you from putting your skills, experience and person-ality over positively. **You need to convince the employer that**

you have a lot to offer the company. Let us think about this from the employer's point of view.

Stressing your contribution

Imagine that you run a company and need to employ an office manager. You already know that *everyone* who applies wants the job, and that it would improve their career prospects should they be successful. You do not necessarily want to hear at the interview how beneficial it would be for the candidates to get the job, because all the applicants will feel the same way. So those candidates who explain at great length how they are looking for exactly this kind of job as it fits very neatly into their career plan, will not impress you.

As the employer you want to hear what the candidates are going to offer *you* and what they can contribute to your organisation. The days have long gone when employers had difficulty in attracting applicants for vacancies. Now, assuming that you have advertised appropriately, you will have a good selection of people applying for your vacancy. Hundreds of applications arrive for some vacancies. The main question that you want answered is: 'Which one of the people I am interviewing today would offer my organisation most as an employee?'

You want candidates to outline what they bring that enables them to be of particular assistance to you. In this example, your questions will be: 'Do the candidates have experience of managerial work that would be helpful to our company? Are their skills relevant and directly transferable to the work that we do? Do they seem as though they have a positive and keen enough attitude to be involved with a company like ours? If we employ them, would they be able to get down to work fairly quickly with the minimum of input from us?' These questions will be going through the mind of any interviewer and they will be far more interested in finding out these answers than hearing all about the needs of the candidates.

Dos and don'ts

✔ Do put yourself in the employer's shoes when thinking about what will work in the interview.

✔ Do spend some time thinking about yourself, your background and your strengths.

✔ Do come up with examples and illustrations to justify the claims you make about yourself.

✘ Don't leave researching the employer and the vacancy too late; it can take time.

✘ Don't get frightened. Allow your interest in the job to let your enthusiasm grow.

✘ Don't tell too many people that you have got an interview in case you do not get the job.

Points to remember

1. Employers are often bad at interviewing people.

2. If you have been called for an interview, you should stand as good a chance as any candidate of getting the job.

3. The truth is that the candidate who performs best on the day will usually get the job.

4. The most important factor to convey is that you are the right sort of person for the job.

5. You need to convince the employer that you have a lot to offer.

Planning and preparation

Importance of planning and preparation

Imagine that you have applied for a job you very much want. Today, 'plop', on to the doormat, comes a letter inviting you for an interview. Congratulations! So far everything you have done has impressed the employer. Now that we have more of an idea of the principles behind the interviewing process, we can look in more detail at what to say. PLANNING and PREPARATION allow you to immerse yourself in the process to give you CONFIDENCE which leads to ENTHUSIASM and SUCCESS.

An essential part of your preparation for attending any interview is deciding in advance your view of yourself, how you see the employer and your ideas about what you will do in the job. This is particularly important if you are being asked to give a presentation as part of the interview. This part of the process of getting ready for an interview could be called research and development: research about the job and how you view it and development of your plan to depict yourself and your strengths.

Your view of yourself

Spend some time thinking about your employment history, especially trying to understand how your background will look when it is being considered through the eyes of an employer. Can you easily identify your transferable skills – that is, those that will directly apply to this job being advertised? What exactly did you do in your last job in terms of practical activities? It is useful to make a preliminary list at this stage to remind yourself how you spent your time in previous jobs. Spend a little time thinking through what went well in these recent jobs, what you achieved and what key abilities you displayed.

As well as being clear about your strengths and skills, you need to be able to explain away any gaps in your CV, or anything that does not tie up convincingly. For instance, you may have had periods when you were neither employed nor studying. If this is the case, it is highly likely that these breaks will be noticed and picked up during an interview, so you need to be able to discuss all of your past without embarrassment. This means making the most of the way you have spent your time. If you were unemployed, what did you spend your time doing? If you were travelling, what did you learn from your experiences in different places? Gaps and breaks will not necessarily be seen as bad or regrettable as long as you can talk through what you experienced in a positive light, particularly pointing out what you learned from them.

How you see the employer

With the wealth of information available in our knowledge economy, there is no excuse for not finding out a great deal about an employer before you attend the interview. An organisation's website is obviously a good place to start. A useful part of your preparation is to discover as much as you can in answer to the following questions:

■ What goods or services does this employer deal with?

■ What are the stated aims and values or mission statement of the organisation, if they exist?

■ If a private sector company, how is it performing and who are its main competitors?

■ If a not-for-profit organisation, how much of a priority is it given currently with funding bodies and political decision-makers?

■ How would you describe what sort of an organisation this is?

■ What kind of skills will they be looking for at the moment?

■ Could you identify the organisation's culture? What do they believe in and how do they run things? How would it feel to work there? There is a huge difference between a traditional, hierarchical institution and a young, dynamic enterprise. In which would you feel most at home? Why is this?

Research

The next stage of planning is to collect all the information you can about the vacancy and the organisation. You will rarely be invited for interview without being given some clues as to the sort of candidate required. If the job was advertised and you have been sent a job description or, even better, a person specification, you have as good as been told most of the areas on which you are likely to be questioned.

A job description, as the name suggests, details the main duties of the job and a person specification explains what sort of person the employer is looking for. Both these documents are very useful. Make sure you pay careful attention to all the paperwork that you receive about the job. The employer will have gone to a lot of time and trouble to write down what the post involves. You will be expected to show evidence that you have a lot to offer for each and every part of it.

Relate your thinking to the research you carried out when initially applying for the post. You need to build on this earlier work and plan out how your background can fit with the skills and experience that are needed for the job. If you do not fit the job description or person specification perfectly, find extra points in your favour that could compensate for these gaps.

Selling yourself

In the past when applicants for positions were much fewer, carefully working through these documents to show that you had the necessary experience and character would have been enough to get you a job. Nowadays, with so much more competition, it is not just a question of paying attention to detail but of finding ways to 'sell yourself'. Such an expression seems to apply more to washing powder than to human beings, but it is a good term to use.

Consider an advertisement for any washing powder on the television. We are not just shown a box of the washing powder and told to buy it. We may be shown a washing line full of sparkling white clothes to demonstrate exactly what the product can do. We are told repeatedly that it washes whiter; gives our clothes a lovely, fresh smell; is substantially cheaper than its rivals; comes in a refillable pack; removes dirt and stains, etc.

Because of all the other advertisements for similar products, the message is hammered home. But when we watch an advert like this, it does not seem as though the message has been too strong; rather, we are left with the impression that it may be a product we ought to try. This is the effect we want to create with the interviewer by using the invited time available to promote our strengths and positive attributes.

Analysing the job
The job description

By looking closely at the details in the job description you can see what the employer expects the job-holder to do. The tasks are sometimes split up into those where some experience is essential and others where experience is preferred. Ideally, you need to go through the following steps:

- Work through the job description, taking one section at a time.

- Underline or mark the words which mention the main activities of the job (the verbs), eg organising work; preparing budgets; writing reports; dealing with customers.

- Make rough notes to show how you have gained experience of all these activities – think of an example from your background or work experience for each one.

- Convert your rough notes into a written or typed form that gives answers to questions on how you satisfy each of the points that you have underlined.

- Revisit the information that you provided on your application form, adding more examples as appropriate, so that you have a stock of different types of evidence to offer.

The person specification

This document is often sent out for vacancies in large companies, local authorities, other public sector employers or the Civil Service, all of which have large human resources departments. It contains useful information about the type of person the organisation is looking for. Your approach to this information should be the same as for the job description:

■ Study it carefully to see what characteristics are either *essential* for the job or *preferred* and underline both.

■ Work through each of these items in rough, noting down an example from your own background which shows how your personality fits closely with what is required. You *must* provide proof that you have all the characteristics marked as essential to be successful in the interview. It is sensible to prepare more than one example in case you are asked for extra.

■ Write your answers in proper sentences so that you can rehearse them for the actual interview.

■ If you completed an application form for this job previously, revisit this now to refresh your memory so you can fully prepare your answers on how you meet the person specification.

How to find out more

You may want to contact the company either formally or informally to find out more about them and what they do. By a formal contact I mean telephoning and talking to the person in charge of personnel or the local manager. For example:

'I have been invited for an interview with your company/ organisation soon and I wondered if there was any more information available about your products/services.'

There may be a specific question that you want answered, such as:

'Are all your offices based around London?'

Some people are happier not revealing that they are coming for an interview and simply say that they are doing research and want some information. Public companies publish annual reports which contain useful background on the major projects undertaken recently.

Companies often advertise their products or services in magazines, local and national newspapers and on the internet. These advertisements can show you how the company presents itself, and tell you which are its main products.

If you are targeting a certain organisation, you can look it up on the internet. Search engines are fast and powerful ways to look up specific information. A good example is www.google.co.uk. You could use it to look up words that relate to particular types of work or to pinpoint information about a specific employer. Most organisations now have their own website, which outlines what they do and how they do it. Comb the site of the employer who will be interviewing you until you know as much as possible about the company. Look carefully at the words and pictures they use to describe themselves. What kind of image are they portraying? Do some serious thinking about what you see. It will not be enough just to say that you have visited the site as that will be expected. You need to form some conclusions of your own. Look too at the websites of other similar organisations, or those of their competitors, as you will find more useful information from these sources.

For some more senior jobs, you may be invited to telephone the company for an informal discussion about the position before applying. If this happens for a job you are thinking about, you should contact the employer to check that your application would be taken seriously. However, you will need to treat this telephone contact as a mini-interview. Look at your CV before you call and have clear in your mind why you think you might be suitable, what specifically interests you about the job and, particularly, what you think you have to offer in the role. If you have any questions, have them prepared in advance, together with pen and paper to take notes during the call.

Thinking about the job

When you are satisfied that you have gathered as much material as possible in the time available, you need to begin thinking hard about the likely subjects to be covered at interview. To start with, though, consider the following advertisement, seen in a local paper:

STOCK HANDLER

Busy high street store requires seasonal stock handlers to work in their warehouse, sorting and checking stock. Training given but experience useful.

Now what can we tell, from this short advertisement, about the person required? Even without a job description or a person specification, and without knowing the name of the company, we can use our common sense to deduce the following. The person will need to be fit and healthy in order to carry boxes of stock around. There is bound to be a certain amount of paperwork and administration, involving completing and checking stock record cards, so the right candidate will need to be literate and numerate. Some knowledge of IT, or at least a willingness to learn, is always going to be useful. Using lifting equipment and/or driving ability may also be relevant for this job.

The store is likely to be a large one if it has its own ware-house, so the work will probably involve working with teams of people. Someone with a friendly and flexible approach is needed. Accuracy will be important and care will have to be taken with the stock because of the value of the goods handled. The candidate should be honest and able to be trusted with valuables.

All these duties and characteristics can be inferred from the brief details given in the advert. We could get much more of an idea of the person required if we had been given a job description and a person specification. But even without them, there is no excuse for not thinking through what the employer is looking for as part of your preparation.

If you are not prepared to do some planning before the event, and do not feel that you can get excited about the vacancy, it may mean that you are not serious about applying for the position. Generally, if a job is worth going for, it is worth spending time preparing for, and that involves sifting through all the information at your disposal for clues about what exactly the employer is looking for. This will help you to form a profile of the candidate most likely to be successful.

Areas of likely questioning

It was stated earlier that an employer will be interested in three main areas of questioning. You know without a doubt that you will be asked questions about: (a) your qualifications and skills; (b) your previous work experience; and (c) your character or personality. Let us look at each of these areas in turn.

(a) Your qualifications and skills

Before you are interviewed it is helpful to have prepared a good CV. This document is useful for interviews as well as job applications as it should contain a concise list of courses taken and jobs held. Before the interview you will need to make a thorough review of your background, especially if you have taken several different courses. Fluffing your answers when you are unsure of your ground is all too apparent to an interviewer and looks unprofessional.

You will then be completely familiar with what you have spent time studying, and where and when. You almost need to be able to recite your CV in your sleep! As a result, when you are asked questions about your educational background, the information you require will come easily and concisely.

When you are being interviewed and are asked about your past studies, the employer does not want to hear you recite a list of the courses you have attended. Think *why* the employer should be interested in such information. The reason is that he or she wants to know *what you learned* from your studies. In most cases, therefore, it is more important to get across the main subjects studied, what projects you specifically worked on, which exams you passed – if any – and which parts of the course you enjoyed most, or learned most from.

Those who have not taken any exams will still be expected to talk about courses studied at school or college. You will need to work out which were your favourite subjects, which lessons you felt benefited you most, and why.

(b) Your previous work experience

The same is true of your work experience. All your jobs and the details of what you did as your main duties need to be at the front of your mind. You should not assume that it is obvious to an interviewer what you did as a filing clerk. Most interviewers will be interested in the precise skills used in the job that could help you to contribute to the position applied for.

You may think that all filing clerks file – but what sort of documents were you dealing with? Were they important legal papers or plans, originals of letters or clients' personal details? Perhaps you used to file things by number rather than alphabetically, or you might have had to cross-reference materials. Did you ever have to retrieve records in a hurry, work under pressure or trace missing papers? Did you ever use particular IT programmes, answer queries from the public or liaise with colleagues from other departments? Were the documents confidential or private or did they need special treatment before filing, eg coding to aid retrieval?

All these things could be what are called *transferable skills*, ie skills that you learn or use in one job which can be transferred to the next. The advantage to an employer should be obvious. Your skill in one area of work, in which you can demonstrate expertise, means that you will not necessarily need training to do the same thing in the next job.

Again, let us consider *why* the interviewer is asking this type of question. The answer is, to see what kind of an employee you would make. Therefore, *when* you worked in a particular place is not as important as *what you contributed there*, since it gives the employer an idea of your capabilities.

(c) Your character or personality

Of the three main areas of interest to an employer, the greatest importance attaches to the type of person you are. It happens again and again; even if a candidate's educational background or previous experience is not up to those of his or her competitors, by demonstrating certain advantages involving personality or character, the candidate is successful in getting the job. Why should this be so? As long as a candidate is the sort of person who will fit into the company and who enjoys his or her work, that person can easily be trained to compensate for any lack of skills or experience.

Sharing the vision

There is one further aspect for employers to consider when they are interviewing. Many candidates may seem to have appropriate qualifications, experience and personality to fit the vacancy. What else could make the difference between the best and the rest? In a downturn, employers may find that they start to attract lots of suitable applicants. They will be looking for ways to pick out the people who are offering them the most. If candidates can show that they have thought about the job, specifically the contribution that they can make and the way that the job should be done, they cannot fail to impress.

This requires spending some time thinking about the key aspects of the job. What are the strengths and weaknesses of the organisation as far as you can tell? What can you discover about the environment in which the company is operating? Think about both the job and the organisation and try to analyse which factors might be important.

For instance, if the vacancy is with a commercial company, who are its competitors? What is your image of the product or service provided? Are there any changes taking place in the wider world that might affect the company's business? What about the nature of the specific job concerned? What do you see as the most important features of the job and why? How do you imagine yourself doing the job and what special contribution would you make?

Spending time developing your ideas or vision about the future for the organisation shows both your commitment to, and interest in, the job and the likely added value that you could bring compared to other candidates. Most employers do not have the time to think about the specific details of every job in their organisation. They want to recruit people who can do the job well on their behalf and bring fresh ideas and energy to the task. You will enhance the impression you make if you can also talk intelligently about your vision of the organisation and how you see your role in it.

Mind the gap! Covering up your weak spots

We all have something we would prefer the interviewer didn't linger over. For some it may be time spent unemployed; for others it may be something in their past that they would prefer to cover up, such as a lot of job changes or having stayed too long in a dead-end job. Few people have a perfect career history, owing to various circumstances, eg having a family, a period of ill-health, previous or current unemployment, imprisonment or detention. Some of us have had periods caring for family members, perhaps elderly parents, or have taken time off to bring up children. You may have left a job in a hurry or feel that your employment history looks patchy and unimpressive. Don't think that if you ignore these tricky issues they will go away. Gaps or inconsistencies in your CV or application form will be spotted and queried. You need to be able to discuss all aspects of your background with confidence and with a positive explanation. No employer will expect you to have sailed through life without hiccoughs or difficulties but you will need to spend some time preparing how you describe and clarify them.

What is important is that you think through and practise how to deal with these gaps. It means learning, not how to lie, but how to put forward positively a cogent and convincing explanation of the relevant experience you have gained in the past.

Maximising your strengths

The best approach is not to cover up past experiences but to present them in a different way. This requires you to make a virtue out of things that happened to you through necessity. Let us look at an example. Imagine someone who has had several different jobs in a short space of time. The best way to justify this is to work out how this will concern an employer.

So let us climb inside the mind of an employer who is faced with an interviewee called Deborah.

Deborah has had six jobs in the last five years and is applying to join W Sayer's company as a personal assistant. Mr Sayer, the managing director, is concerned that, as Deborah has had many different jobs, she may want to leave this job in a few months' time. If that happened he would have to repeat the expensive and time-consuming task of selecting another employee. He is worried too that she will not settle into the position, that she will not take the work seriously and that she will not show enough commitment to the company.

Deborah realises that these job changes are something she should present positively to the interviewer. She does not imply that she was unhappy in any of her previous jobs but suggests that, even if she did not stay long in any one position, the employers were glad to have had her working there even for a limited time because of the contribution she was able to make.

She spends time before the interview thinking about what she contributed in each of her previous jobs and what it was that made her want to move each time. In other words, she worked out her story in advance and planned what information she wanted to convey in the interview.

Golden rules

1. Always be positive about previous jobs
It is important always to be positive about *every* job that you have had in the past. Why should this be so vital? Again, let us consider it from the employer's point of view. Will it impress an interviewer to hear a candidate saying what a bad boss his or her last employer was? Will it sound good to hear another company being put down or maligned by a candidate, or will it make the employer think that the candidate could

well be saying the same sort of thing about this company in a few years' time?

Someone who moans about other organisations also creates an impression of surliness and a negative attitude. Nobody will be interested in employing such a candidate. A candidate who is positive and keen will be preferred.

2. Be enthusiastic and motivated

Nothing attracts people like enthusiasm. The candidate who exhibits such a characteristic has a great advantage, almost before anything else is said or taken into consideration. We are all more interested in working with the person who comes into work each day in a good mood and feeling positive about the job, rather than with the moaner or troublemaker who is always being negative.

3. Capitalise on your strengths

The only things that the interviewer knows about you are what you have put in your application or CV and what you are going to talk about in the actual interview. Therefore, what you say about yourself dictates the impression that the interviewer will have of you, ie your skills, experience and personality. The interviewer will be looking at you as a potential worker or member of staff – you need to imply that everything you have been doing so far has been leading up to this job, with this organisation, at this time. Couple that with your vision of the way the job should be handled from now on. Irresistible!

Which questions to ask?

At the end of the interview, you will usually be asked if you have any questions to put. Do not feel obliged to ask something just for the sake of it. The employer's heart will sink if you start to reel off a long list of questions just when the interview should be ending. Only ask a question if it is necessary. If you feel that you know all you need to about the job on offer, it is fine to say something like:

'I think that you have covered all the important points already, thank you. But if I have any questions later I will contact you.'

Do not ask questions about uniforms, holidays or other practical points. If you are offered the post you will be informed about this kind of detail when you start.

If pay has not been mentioned so far, this is not the time to raise the issue. You would probably not accept any position without knowing the wages, but again you can find this out once you receive the offer of the job, when you could reply:

'I am interested in the job at this stage, but I am still not quite sure about the conditions of employment. Can you tell me exactly what the wages and hours are?'

If you do decide to ask the interviewer some questions, it is a good idea to show your general attitude through what you say. Questions about training opportunities or the chance to take on greater responsibilities in the future show that you are keen, plan to stay in the job, and are interested in moving up the organisation.

You could ask: 'Would there be opportunities for more specialist work later on?' or 'Could you tell me a little about what personal development you support for your employees?'

Dos and Don'ts

✔ Do use new technology and the internet to give you an advantage when researching.

✔ Do start with revising what you put in your application – it is what has secured you the interview.

✔ Do think about the kind of person the employer will be looking for.

✘ Don't leave research until the last minute – you may need more time than you realise.

✘ Don't worry if you do not seem to fit the vacancy in every way – you may be just what they are looking for.

✘ Don't forget to prepare examples of all the points they are asking for.

Points to remember

1. Studying the paperwork available about the job pays dividends.

2. Think yourself into the job, so that you talk as if you are doing it already.

3. Concentrate on what makes you more employable than the other candidates.

4. Try to make links between your past experience and what is needed in this role.

5. Turn negative aspects of your past into positives by stressing what you learned or how an episode developed your character.

Creating the best impression

The importance of personal image

You may be asking why a chapter in a book on interviewing skills should be about personal image. Surely the most important thing to learn is what to say in the interview? On the contrary, the impression we make on other people consists of much more than just the words we speak. A large part of the way we judge other people comes from first impressions. In other words, what we notice in the first quick glance, which may last for only 30 seconds, is the way other people look and behave.

In fact, research has shown that 55 per cent of this first impression is based on appearance and behaviour, which can include clothing, posture, body language and facial expressions. Thirty-eight per cent of the impression is from the way we speak, which includes the way the voice is used, clarity of speech and accent. Only seven per cent is from the words we say.

Just consider this startling information for a moment. It means that a whole 93 per cent of that all-important first impression we make on other people is rooted in *what we look like and the way we sound*. We live in an ever more televisual age where our information on what is happening in the world tends to come from a talking head and shoulders on the TV set. As a result we have become increasingly sophisticated in the level of presentation we expect and the degree to which we home in on distractions and inconsistencies. We have strong preferences for what we do and do not like. However, this is not information to be depressed about; on the contrary, it gives us much more control over the extent to which we can impress other people, especially interviewers.

So whenever you are preparing for an interview it is necessary to spend a significant amount of time evaluating and considering the best way to present yourself physically to the employer.

Creating a positive first impression

If you are now saying that you personally do not judge others by such superficial measures, consider the importance of visual image when you next meet people for the first time. Imagine you are at a party and want to make some new friends. Looking round the room, you notice someone whom you have not met before. She looks a bit dowdy and is standing alone with a worried expression on her face. She is looking at the floor with her shoulders slightly hunched and her arms folded tightly across her front. Although someone is trying to talk to her, she does not seem to be contributing much to the conversation.

Now you notice somebody else. She is smartly dressed, has a twinkle in her eye and is chatting animatedly to someone. She has just grinned at you in a friendly way, and you notice that she is standing up tall and looking confident. Which one of these two people would you be most likely to talk to?

The impression we gain about the first woman in this example is that she looks as though she does not care about herself much. She is not dressed up for a party and she appears uncomfortable and ill at ease as if she lacks self-confidence. The fact that she is not engaging in conversation may mean that she is avoiding contact with new people or just that she does not have much to talk about.

Now, of course, this opinion may be completely wrong. For all we know she may be a Hollywood star just back from a major film shoot, who is dressing down for the evening as a reaction to spending the last two months in film costume and theatrical make-up. She may be quiet and withdrawn because she only wants to meet new and genuine friends, not hangers-on. However, we are distracted by the contrast between her and the second woman in our example.

The second woman seems to be inviting attention and contact. She is outward-focused, noticing the people around her and encouraging you by smiling in your direction. She appears to be a worthwhile person to try chatting to.

If we act on our positive first impressions of this person and start chatting to her, during our subsequent conversation at the party we may find out that she is a rather forlorn, needy egomaniac, but we would not assume this from her initial appearance.

In other words, we are highly affected by our visual impressions of others, particularly where rapid decisions have to be made (and an hour-long job interview is a fairly short time in which to decide on the best candidate). We will make judgements about the merits and demerits of people by picking up any visual clues we can – especially if certain individuals in a group stand out.

Even though we may not like to think that we are being judged by others on their first impression of us, we are doing exactly the same to other people all the time. We all have prejudices about what we like to look at and what sort of behaviour we think is appropriate at different times. The secret of success is in understanding how other people perceive you and then using this information to your advantage. Interviewers will make many allowances for a well-presented candidate.

The information in this chapter will be useful in many situations – not just at interviews. Once you know how to create a good first impression, you can be that person at the party whom everyone wants to meet. But creating a good first impression at an interview is doubly important because so much is at stake when you meet potential employers.

It is your responsibility to make sure that the impression you create works in your favour. This does not mean trying to put on an act or pretending to be someone else, as this will be obvious to the interviewer; rather, you want to enhance your strong points and minimise your weaker ones. You may not get a job on image alone but it can certainly help.

Research suggests that 55 per cent of first impressions are created by the way we look and behave, 38 per cent by the way we sound and only 7 per cent by what we say. Let us look at each of these areas in turn. We will start by considering the factors that comprise the first two of these: appearance and voice. What you actually say in the interview is analysed in Chapter 6.

Appearance

I make no apology for concentrating on your physical appearance as part of your interview preparation. It can have a highly significant effect on your chances of getting a job. My aim is to get you to spend at least as much time on this aspect of your presentation as you do rehearsing your interview answers. In the same way as the costume and stage make-up are pivotal to the impression of the actor on the stage, you are also going to be performing. You will have a short space of time, in competition with others, to make your mark. It makes sense to use everything at your disposal.

Many more jobs have been lost by conveying a too casual attitude to the vacancy through appearance and body language than through providing one less-good answer. Our aim here is not to win a beauty contest but to ensure that our appearance is just right, that it provides no distractions and allows the interviewer to concentrate on our skills, aptitudes and personality in relation to the job.

Your appearance is the most important aspect of the first impression you create. This cannot be stressed too much, and if it is the only thing you learn from reading this book, it will be valuable. The advice in this section applies equally to men and women. A smart appearance shows that you have taken trouble over the way you want to come across. A plain neutral look indicates a serious, professional outlook. Your choice of clothes indicates your attitude to yourself and other people.

It is worth thinking about the kind of appearance that is expected in the kind of job you are applying for. In creative industries the look is generally much more individualistic and casual. Men often do not wear suits to the office. In more traditional sectors such as banking or the legal profession, the work clothing is also more traditional and suits are more prevalent, even for women staff, with more of a uniform appearance for all.

In the middle range comes employment such as teaching, local authority work and personal services that tend to exhibit more formality of appearance at the senior levels and a more casual look for junior staff. Once you have decided what the normal 'dress code' is for the kind of work you are applying for, you can choose your interview clothes by pitching your look one step up from the norm. For instance, you may decide to attend a job interview for a lecturing position in a suit whereas you would only wear a matching jacket and trousers or skirt for a clerical position in a museum.

Women will be more familiar with the points made here because they tend to be exposed to more advice and information about appearance than men, but this generally leads merely to lack of confidence. Being bombarded with messages about fashion and advertisements from the clothing and cosmetics industries only serves to worry women. It is similar to being spoilt for choice in a larger supermarket compared to the relatively simple choices of a corner shop – the shopping experience in the supermarket can lead to confusion. Interviews are difficult enough without adding the burden of concern about our appearance. The aim here is to eradicate this particular anxiety.

You do not want to appear showy or quirky in your choice of clothes but you should look clean and smart. I am often asked whether it is possible to be overdressed for an interview. I do not think so (with the possible exception of a dinner jacket or ball gown!). Even if the job would normally require you to wear overalls or a uniform, dressing with care for your interview shows you have taken time over your appearance and indicates an awareness of being, to some extent, on show. For instance, a candidate for a motor mechanic traineeship may well want to wear a suit or jacket, tie and shirt to the interview at least, even if overalls would be worn once doing the job.

Men should wear a dark suit, or at least a smart jacket and tie for a job where less formal clothing is the norm. Women should dress smartly (a jacket is a good idea), and not be cluttered with accessories. Whatever the job, it is helpful when you are feeling nervous to add authority to the impression you create.

Colour and style of clothes

It is generally acknowledged that there is a particular range of colours that suits an individual best. These colours will be different for everybody but can help to give each of us a distinct presence. The right clothes do not draw attention to themselves; rather, they show off the person inside them, and in the right colours you will receive compliments on how well you are looking rather than on your clothes. Looking your best does not involve spending a lot of money on clothes, wearing the latest fashions or trying to look like someone else. A classic single-breasted jacket that you look after will not date. If you have no money, see if you can borrow clothes from a friend or relative but do not squeeze yourself into something too small. Wearing clothes that are too tight merely makes you look bigger; if in doubt use a size larger than normal to make you look smaller. Add height with accessories that accentuate the upper half of your body, such as a brooch or noticeable earrings.

As a rule, plain neutral colours are safest when you want to look smart. Navy blue or medium to dark grey for suits or jackets and a contrasting soft (not bright) white or ivory shirt or blouse work well for a confident, competent appearance. Black looks best on those with strong natural colouring or dark hair.

Don't confuse looking attractive or pretty with looking business-like. If you have long flowing hair, consider tying it back neatly for the interview to look more disciplined and practical. Women should avoid wearing low-cut, tight-fitting or otherwise revealing clothes. Keep your clothes that get attention for your social life and let your abilities and ideas do the talking in the interview.

Image consultants give professional advice on the colour and style of clothes to suit your natural colouring and body shape. The advice given is based on the idea of tailoring the colours you wear to those in the natural colouring of your hair, eyes and skin. The same applies to the style of your clothes. You have a certain body shape which can be echoed in your clothes to show you to your best advantage. This applies to a greater extent to women because of the more extensive range of styles and colours available to them, but it is also relevant to men – in particular to the shape and style of their clothes.

Accessories

Ties, shoes, belts, bags and jewellery can make or break an outfit, although we tend to think of them as additions to our general look. Shoes are often noticed and should be appropriate, clean and smart for an interview. An employer I know says he looks first at a candidate's footwear. 'You can tell a lot about a person from their choice and care of shoes,' he says. 'The shoes don't have to be new but I'm always impressed if they are smart, well-looked after and clean. I would advise people to invest in a good pair of leather shoes because good quality shows.' This employer's field is public relations and he judges candidates' ability to present themselves as a good pointer to the way they would behave in the job. Dangling earrings should be left for evening wear, as should jingly bracelets. Jewellery is not generally considered acceptable on men and so it should be removed for the duration of the interview. Men should wear socks and shoes to match their suit. Make sure your socks are long enough not to reveal expanses of skin if sitting with your legs crossed. Women should carry only one bag, if you need one at all. If you take a briefcase, put your handbag items in it. Don't juggle with both a briefcase and a handbag as it detracts from a well-organised, authoritative image.

Hair

Your hair should be clean and recently cut. If you do this about a week before the interview, you will have time to get used to your new haircut. Most people look best with their natural hair colour, and this is evident when they are wearing clothes to complement their natural colouring.

Make-up

If you wear make-up, make sure that the style and colour do not date you. This is another area where women often lack confidence, because they are bombarded with conflicting advice from advertisements and magazine articles, but they do not seek specialist help. Again, one trip to an image consultant can solve these problems and you will be given advice on the best colours and style of make-up to suit you.

If the interview is important to you, it is worth taking the time and trouble to be neat, clean and well groomed. Make sure that your hands are clean and your nails neat. There is also no point in wearing smart clothes if they are not clean. Shirts or blouses that have not been ironed are particularly noticeable and create a sloppy look, regardless of how attractive they are. Body odour or greasy hair are not ways to impress any employer. Ask a trusted friend or relative to assess you for cleanliness and smartness. If in any doubt, use a deodorant.

Behaviour

There are many books in your local library which will tell you about the scientific study of body language and non-verbal communication. Basically, we are all animals and respond to each other on a simple level in this way. When we meet other animals we need to know that we are not under threat. That is why *smiling* at another human being is such a powerful signal.

When we smile at other people we reassure them that we are not going to attack them, and being smiled at by others is the way *we* receive reassurance that the person facing us is not an enemy. Communication between people is much more relaxed and straightforward when we know we are safe. Think about how difficult it is to make conversation with your dentist before you have treatment. So, to create a good impression, start off the interview on a positive note by entering the room and smiling at all the interviewers present. Even if you are too scared to smile again, you will have started the interview in a confident way. Shaking the hands of those who will be interviewing you is a helpful way to start if you feel confident in doing so. Obviously, if a cumbersome table blocks the way between you and a large number of interviewers, attempting to shake hands may cause more trouble than it will be worth, but if possible, a firm, friendly handshake makes you look open and positive. This applies particularly to women who can make an impact this way through rarity value, as shaking hands is still less common amongst women.

At the end of the interview when you leave, make sure you thank the interviewers for the time and attention you have been afforded and smile again to leave on the same positive note. If you began by shaking hands, leave the same way.

Eye contact

Looking straight into somebody's eyes when we are talking tells the person that we are interested, attending to what is being said and have nothing to hide. When we feel shy, it is sometimes awkward to keep this direct gaze on the interviewer. If you find this difficult, at least try to look at the interviewer when he or she is asking you a question, even if you look elsewhere during your response. If you are being interviewed by more than one person, do not always try to include everyone in the panel in your glance. Instead, when one interviewer asks you an individual question, treat that person as though he or she is the only one interviewing you.

You should ensure that your behaviour cannot be perceived as flirtatious. This is not part of any job description and if your behaviour seems inappropriate, it could work against you and you may not be taken seriously as a candidate.

Posture

Other important aspects of body language for an interview are those relating to posture. You want to attract attention and be remembered. You must walk tall with your shoulders back, pulling yourself up by the head to increase your height and make your spine straight. You will look around you in an alert way and meet any other person's gaze directly, while smiling confidently at everyone you meet.

In the interview, you do not want to appear insignificant or unremarkable. You want the interview panel to be left with a striking and positive impression of you physically.

When you sit down in the interview, make sure that your bottom is set well back on the seat, with your spine held fairly straight and supported by the back of the chair. Leaning forward slightly gives an impression of keenness. Do not slouch or sprawl in your seat – it implies that you are not taking the interview seriously. Practise in advance to find out which seating position is most comfortable for you. It does not matter whether your legs are crossed or not, but do not keep changing their position or you will distract the interviewer from what you are saying.

Gestures

Hands should be lightly clasped in your lap or can rest on the arms of your chair. Gestures add variety to speech, and your natural style may be to use your hands in this way occasionally. Too much gesticulation implies anxiety and tension, so monitor this when you are practising your answers in front of the mirror.

Confidence

Confidence has been mentioned before as though it should be easy to acquire. Everybody is confident about their abilities in some activity or other. If I asked you to tell me something that you felt confident about, it could be cookery, playing sport or a hobby. If you analyse *why* you are confident at that particular activity, what would you attribute it to? Are you confident because it is a familiar task; because you have been told that you are good at it; because you are well prepared; or because you have studied how to do it?

Often, all these reasons apply, and that is why practising your interview technique is so valuable. Half the terror of an impending interview is because you do not know what to expect. Rehearsing in advance means that you will feel reassured about which questions may come up, and about your ability to answer them.

Increase your confidence by preparing thoroughly, packing carefully any items you might need if you are going to give a presentation, eg hand-outs or flip-chart pens.

Positive mental attitude

Often when going for interviews, candidates are too aware of why they might not be successful. Some of the most common reasons for getting in a negative state of mind are that you feel:

■ it is years since you have been tested at an interview;

■ you have failed other interviews recently;

■ you are desperate to leave your current job;

■ you may be too keen to get this job and so feel very worried;

■ you may not be really clear what you are looking for;

■ you may be deeply demotivated by your career prospects and feel you have nothing to offer.

None of these attitudes will help you to be successful at interview so it is important to convert negative thoughts to more constructive ones. You can set your own mental attitude to positive instead of negative. Sports stars claim that the most significant factor in winning is their mental approach to the event. In addition to training and fitness, they need to feel like a winner in order to act like one. We have much more influence over our own thoughts and feelings than you might think. Imagine a day when you are feeling down when out of the blue someone delivers a bouquet of flowers or a present to the door for you. Immediately your world seems brighter and your mood becomes more positive. This quick change can be brought about at other times by changing the way you are thinking too.

First you need to concentrate deliberately on boosting yourself up. Although we all have disappointments and difficulties during our lives, there are also lots of achievements and successes that we can claim.

Spend a few minutes considering each of the following points:

You achieve successfully in several areas of your life already: relationships, keeping your domestic life running, family contacts, holding down a job (if you have one), keeping a nice home going, planning the things you want.

list some more here:

_____
_____
_____

People are impressed by you as an interesting and valuable person: employers who have hired you in the past, family and friends, colleagues, social contacts, lovers and partners.

list some of them here:

_____
_____
_____

You can get things when you want to: support from friends, praise from family, attention from loved ones, cooperation from colleagues, being promoted (if you ever have been).

list some more here:

_____

_____

_____

Now reflect on that exercise. You have put together evidence of your success in all of these areas. Altogether you are a successful, valuable and interesting person. Still need a bit of convincing? Go out for a walk and think about all the things on this list in more detail. Visualisation can be a powerful tool to use. Re-visit the best times in your life and what you were doing at the time that made them so good. Those times were substantially your doing and it was your personality that helped them to happen. Try to fix an image in your mind of a time or event when you were doing well and felt at your best, so that you can conjure it up again whenever you need to feel good about yourself. Imagine the people who love you most are cheering you on. What would they be saying to you, and about you?

Starting to think about any approaching interview in this frame of mind automatically gives you a head start because you have put your natural doubts to the back of your mind and brought a winning attitude to the fore. When you plan your answers you need to stay in this mindset and, most importantly, replicate it when you walk into the interview room.

Talk to any high achievers, from supermodels to corporate leaders, and they will all say that they have their private worries and stresses, but that they incorporate a positive vision of what they want to achieve and then concentrate on how they can get it to focus them on success. This kind of mental exercise can work just as well for you too.

The journey

The journey to the interview can be a source of anxiety. Plan in advance how much time to allow. If possible, do a 'dummy' or practice run and make sure that you can find the right building and the correct entrance to use. Allow extra time for unforeseen hold-ups. It is important to be on time for your interview, so plan to arrive at least 15 minutes early. Even for the most casual of arrangements, being late can seriously annoy your interviewer. Interviews are normally tightly scheduled so one person being late can throw the whole day's timetable off. If you are delayed for any reason, telephone to let the company know and inform them of your expected time of arrival – although if you arrive too late you may miss the chance of being interviewed altogether.

When you arrive, visit the toilet, check how you look, then forget all about your appearance. Remember that *everybody* you talk to at the company may be asked for their opinion of you – including the doorman, the receptionist and the person who brings you your cup of coffee. I know of a candidate who was only successful because he was friendly and chatty to the office administrator whilst waiting to go in to his interview. The panel could not decide between two equally ranked candidates. They gave the casting vote to someone who had met both just before their interviews – yes, the office administrator.

Voice

Interview nerves affect people in different ways. Some people speak very softly, some talk too fast and start gabbling, others become hesitant and leave long gaps between words. Some people stammer under pressure and some just answer briefly, replying 'yes' or 'no' whenever possible, rather than speaking up about themselves. None of these responses is helpful in an interview.

We have already noted that the whole purpose of your being invited along is for the interviewer to find out as much as possible about you in the time available. Short, quiet, babbled or hesitant answers will not suffice. Of course, any experienced interviewer will make allowances for initial nerves, but will expect you to settle down to the task in hand fairly quickly.

In the interview, just try to imagine that you are talking to someone you know fairly well, and speak in a relaxed and easy manner. Normally, the longer you worry about getting every word and phrase exactly right, the more tangled up you become. Pauses sound fine as part of ordinary speech and are preferable to 'ums' and 'ers'. Pauses only become a problem if they are excessively long, in which case an interviewer may not realise when you have finished speaking. If you know that you are prone to leaving such gaps in the conversation, you could mark the end of your answer by saying something like: 'Those are the main points that I want to make.'

Many of us speak with a regional accent of some kind. It is one of the things about ourselves that we cannot change, or at least not without a great deal of effort. Do not feel self-conscious about the way you speak. It is an important part of who you are and different accents add variety and interest to the way we sound. However, if you are worried that your accent may mean that you are not understood in interviews, try to enunciate clearly, speak slowly and limit your use of local words and phrases if their meaning will not be clear outside your own community.

Controlling nerves

Everybody suffers from nervous feelings in high anxiety situations. This nervous energy provides us with the extra impulse we need in order to put ourselves forward, speak up and perform impressively at an interview. Some of our greatest actors are actually sick before every appearance or the stage, showing that the energy which is generated by nervous tension is crucial to giving a good performance.

When we feel nervous our bodies are reacting to the fact that the forthcoming event is important to us. We have spent time and trouble preparing and rehearsing for the interview and we are getting our response mechanism ready either to go into battle or flee. This is known as the 'fight or flight' mechanism. It is a throwback to the times when we had to either fight our way out of trouble or run away when faced with a threat in the wild, in order to survive. Today we need to harness our nerves to make sure we fight, or at least engage impressively with the interview, rather than panic and dry up. The trick is to make your nervous tension work *for* you, rather than against you. When your nerves work for you, you feel extra alive, highly conscious of everything that is happening around you, very focused on the task in hand and excited by the prospect of the performance ahead.

In any life, there will be many occasions which will bring on an attack of nerves and knowing how to control it will always come in useful. The main antidote is to concentrate on your long-term goal and let this carry you through difficult experiences. So at an interview you need to keep strongly in your mind how important it is that you speak up for yourself and give the interviewer a proper chance to get to know you. Focusing on the point of the event will give you a higher purpose that will enable you to rise above your physical feelings of nervousness. Like the actors who force themselves on to the stage because the show must go on, you can talk and impress people despite your nerves if you keep the purpose of the interview firmly in your mind.

You have been invited to this interview so that the employer can find out about you, and you are going to tell the interviewer all about yourself. If you have prepared well for the interview, you will have thought through how your experience ties in with what the employer is looking for and you will feel excited and enthusiastic about the idea of what you can contribute to the organisation.

This energy you have generated will carry you through the interview, and all the interviewer will remember about you will be your keenness and enthusiasm for the position rather than your nerves.

I once interviewed a series of people for a job requiring energy and commitment. Each one seemed competent and suitable, but none stood out, and I knew it would be difficult to select one to give the job to. At the end of the last interview, the candidate said goodbye with the words: 'I would really love doing this job, you know.' Her obvious enthusiasm shone through her nervousness and I offered her the job on the spot, confident that she was the best candidate. Showing enthusiasm does not mean being immature or sounding desperate to get a job. It requires a genuinely positive attitude to the challenges and opportunities that the vacancy offers.

Your nervousness does not show to other people as much as you think. I run workshops to prepare people for interviews where I make everybody do a mock interview in front of the whole group. Every single person admits to being terribly nervous, but the group is always amazed that each interviewee seems calms and collected. Nerves just do not show. We may know that our palms are sweaty, our stomachs churning and our knees knocking, but no one else will realise our predicament. Fidgeting with coins in a pocket, twiddling strands of hair, constantly touching face or mouth are just some of the ways in which we show our nervousness and we are often unaware of such habits. When an attack of nerves strikes, the energy generated often escapes in repetitive gestures or mannerisms.

Hands are best kept under control, clasped lightly together in your lap. A good way to learn about nervous mannerisms is to ask yourself some of the practice questions which start on page 83, whilst watching your reflection in a mirror. This is your chance to see yourself as others see you. Alternatively, you could ask a friend or relative to give you some honest feedback on your behaviour under pressure.

No self-respecting actor would go on to the stage without adequate rehearsal time, some of it in full dress for the part. Interviews have elements of performance about them which makes them similar to acting. You should have prepared your answers as you want to have a big impact on the audience, so you must learn your 'part' as thoroughly as possible. Practice gives you the chance to do this as well as helping to minimise your nerves. Having rehearsal time with a friend, which involves you answering interview-style questions, can be a great help and feels very different to merely thinking about the answers in your head.

Try to make your rehearsal as realistic as you can, wearing your interview clothes if possible as this run-through will help you to feel more comfortable on the day itself. Tell your friend just to ask you some questions – you could use the sample ones in this book. If they want to give you feedback, ask them to tell you only what they think you did well and how you could make this even better – in other words, get positive feedback only.

On the day the interviewer may also be experiencing some feelings of nervousness. Many managers have little experience or skill at conducting interviews. It is still rare for interviewers to have had any training for the role, particularly in small companies. Most of these employers just muddle through, trying to use common sense in a difficult situation. Moreover, in a panel interview there may be all sorts of tension between the representative from the personnel department, the line manager and the other members of the group of which you will not be aware.

Imagine that you have been asked to interview some job candidates. How would you feel? Perhaps a little apprehensive in advance and on the shaky side when the very first candidate comes into the room? You have never met this person before. Would you be totally confident about what to say and how to handle the candidates? Interviewing is a difficult task because it is stressful to be faced with someone whom we have to talk to in some depth but do not know.

Even asking questions can be difficult for interviewers. You may think that this is a simple task but it is often the case that interviewers, through a lack of skill and experience, tend to ask questions in ways that make them difficult to answer. If you are asked a question such as: 'Did you enjoy your time at college?', please do not just answer 'yes' or 'no', even though that is what the question seems to be looking for. The person asking really wants to know what kind of experience you had at college, what you felt you learned there and if there was anything in particular that would be useful in the job that you are being interviewed for.

Similarly, if you are asked: 'Tell me about your last job, what you achieved there and anything you think would be relevant experience for this job', do not get flummoxed by the fact that this is really three questions in one. Multiple questions like this just show the questioner's eagerness to hear from you; they are not intended to trip you up. Mostly they are asked because the interviewer has not prepared properly for meeting you and their own nervousness makes them phrase their questions in too complicated a way.

Relax and take each part of the question one at a time. You could answer: 'Well, if I start by telling you about the details of the job...' Then you can move on to: 'I think my main achievements there were...' You can finish with: 'My most relevant experiences there as far as this job is concerned include...' If you get lost in the middle, don't feel at all worried about asking; 'Could you just remind me what you asked in the last part of the question please?' After all, if they ask you three questions in one, it is easy to forget some of it.

It is comforting to know that most interviewers are nervous. An interview can be a disquieting experience for the people on both sides of the table. Several employers have confessed to me how much they dread having to interview for staff as they find it very stressful. Remember this next time you attend an interview, take pity on the poor employer and concentrate on putting them at their ease. You do this by showing you are pleased to be there, happy to talk to them and interested in finding out more about the job on offer.

Make sure that you visit the toilet before the interview and do not drink or take drugs to calm you down. They may give you more courage but they will also both impair your performance, and alcohol can always be smelt on the breath.

Relaxation exercises

When you are feeling at your most nervous, you are at the mercy of many different physical symptoms which can seriously derail you from performing well in your interview. However, there are several exercises that you can do to help counter the effects of fear and dread. When we are experiencing the fight or flight mechanism, the body produces adrenalin to help us act to fight or flee from the threat facing us. Adrenalin gets our pulses racing by raising our heart rate ready for action. The body cuts off oxygen from the brain and the extremities, such as the hands and feet. After all, if you are engaged in a fight or running for your life, you do not need to think great thoughts or use tiny hand gestures. All available oxygen is being channelled to our muscles, ready for the fight or the flight that is to ensue. Our hands and feet feel numb and tingly as a result and our minds go blank. We cannot hear properly, sometimes we feel we cannot even see straight and it is difficult to concentrate on what we are trying to say.

All these things are the result of the physical reactions of our body to a perceived threat, so you should not feel a failure if you feel nervous at times like this. Your churning stomach, clammy palms, sweating and confusion are rational reactions to a scary situation. However, a job interview is not a real threat; it is an opportunity, so we need to counter these reactions by taking control of what is happening to us physically. At a time like this we do not need powered-up arms and legs and a blank brain; we need the opposite – a calm body and powered-up mental faculties.

Breathing exercise

Breathing exercises are one way of managing feelings of nervousness. When we are under strain our breathing is likely to become shallow and we do not use all our lung capacity. The effect is to starve the brain of the vital oxygen it needs in order for you to think quickly and clearly. To counteract this you need to do some deeper breathing. Just before you enter the interview room, take several deep breaths. Inhale slowly, standing up if possible, breathe in through your nose and try to fill your lungs completely. See your stomach move out as you fill up with air. Hold this breath for a count of three, then exhale slowly through your mouth. Concentrate on expelling all of the air that you took in. Feel your shoulders relax and watch your stomach flatten as the air is sent out. Repeat for three or four deep breaths only. This will flood your system with oxygen which will counter the unhelpful effects of the flight or fight mechanism.

This exercise should be carried out only in a gentle and rhythmic manner. Do not take it all too far – you do not want to start hyperventilating just as you are called in to your interview! If it is impossible to get some time on your own before your interview, just sit quietly and do your three or four deep breaths in the waiting room. No-one should notice.

Anyway, the other candidates will all be too nervous on their own account to worry about what on earth you are doing.

It can happen that you feel yourself drying up in the middle of the interview and you suddenly feel that you really cannot speak at all or remember your answers or even think. If this occurs, try not to panic as it does not mean that you will inevitably fail the interview. You are simply running short of oxygen and the immediate remedy is to breathe slowly until your brain re-engages. Pause and breathe deeply. Your hesitation will not seem too obvious to the interviewer if you do it confidently. After a couple of breaths you will find everything clicks in to place again and you will be able to continue.

Nerves affect everyone to some degree in interviews. I interviewed someone recently for a job working with children. He was a good candidate on paper but when we met he was unable to answer two of the questions he was asked. He just went completely blank in the interview. He asked if he could come back to these questions later. He was feeling cooler by the end of the interview and answered them adequately at that point. He was mortified though and apologised several times for being so badly affected by his nerves. He was astonished to be offered the job later, as he felt sure that he had thrown away all chance of the job through his hesitation in answering all the questions. In fact, his suitability still shone through and he was easily identifiable as the best candidate – despite his nervousness in the interview. All candidates come across with a certain degree of nerves in interviews and interviewers make allowances for this as long as you try your best to speak up about yourself.

Taking some deep breaths is a very powerful way to handle nerves in any situation whether it is at a social event, before medical treatment, during college exams or any time that you feel scared. In the middle of a recent piano exam, I found my hands shaking uncontrollably and my mind unable to concentrate on the notes. I was unable to play at all. I fought my feelings of panic, told myself to breathe and soon the shaking stopped. Slowly my mind cleared and the notes in front of me came back into focus. I started playing again and passed the exam. The examiner told me afterwards that such attacks of nerves are very common and that I had controlled mine well, not to let it wreck the exam. Even if the situation looks as if it is going badly, you can still retrieve it and do better than you think. Attacks of nerves will happen to all of us but you can stop them from ruining your chances.

Facial exercise

Smiling has another benefit as well as putting the interviewer at ease. It is also an effective way of exercising your facial muscles around the mouth. When we tense up, we take on a stony expression as the muscles contract and a frown of concentration comes over our face. To relax your face, say the vowel sounds aaaa, eeee, iiii, oooo and uuuu and as you do so, gently stretch your mouth in an exaggerated manner around the sounds. Open your mouth wide for aaaa, eeee and iiii, purse your lips tightly together for oooo and uuuu. Repeat this exercise a couple of times and your mouth will flex and get a full work-out as you do it. Finish off with a big wide grin. Make sure that you are on your own as you contort your face to do this exercise or you could seriously alarm anyone watching you!

Dos and don'ts

✔ Do keep focused.

✔ Do wear smart but comfortable clothes.

✔ Do check your appearance before you enter the interview.

✗ Don't take your worries into the interview – go in ready to shine.

✗ Don't fidget – try to sit calmly.

✗ Don't talk too fast because of nerves; pause often.

Points to remember

1. Take time to do some deep breathing, the facial exercise a-e-i-o-u and to *smile*.

2. Keep in the forefront of your mind what you want to achieve.

3. Feel determined about what you want to say.

4. Bear in mind that the interviewer is probably under some strain too.

5. Nerves never show as much as you think.

Making a presentation

Giving a presentation

Sometimes you will be asked to give a presentation as part of the interview. This will not normally be sprung on you. The employer will explain what is required when you receive your invitation to the interview. If it is not clear what you will have to do, do not hesitate to contact the employer to ask for more information. Presentations increasingly form part of the interview as public speaking is involved in many jobs. Some jobs are frequently involved with speaking to groups of people. Some examples of these types of jobs are public relations assistants, training officers or marketing executives. Many other jobs will require you to make a presentation occasionally, to team members, outside visitors or to groups of colleagues. In addition, any managerial or supervisory job will often involve talking to groups of staff and an employer may use a presentation to test your confidence in standing up in front of a group to see how you perform. Employers will be interested to see how well you can direct and lead a group and provide opportunities for group participation if relevant.

Another reason for getting candidates to give a presentation, even if this is not a major part of the job, is that it enables a large amount of information to be given to the interviewer by each candidate. A five or ten minute presentation about why you think you are the best candidate for the job will replace the need for half an hour of questions on the same topic. This means that you get the chance to make your case in whichever way you like. You can decide how to present yourself in the best light to the potential employer. From the employer's point of view, it means that candidates can be compared talking about the same general subjects in each presentation and the interview itself can be used for more searching questions.

Some interviews may require you to do a presentation with no prior information. In this case you are usually given some time to prepare just before you have to give the presentation. This will be to test how well you can think on your feet, select and present material at short notice and keep your cool under pressure.

Planning your presentation

You are being asked to give a presentation to explore how well you can:

■ plan your ideas logically;

■ arrange material in a concise manner;

■ explain key points;

■ present with clarity;

■ have an impact on an audience.

A good presentation needs planning and rehearsal time to be confidently executed. Don't make the mistake of thinking that you can speak off the cuff without at least as much preparation as you give to your answers to the interview questions that may crop up. Even if you are speaking on a topic that you know well, it takes time to put your ideas together clearly and logically. Under time pressure and feeling nervous on the day it is surprising how, unless you have prepared well, your mind can go blank and you can find yourself floundering.

Your task is made easier if you have been told the topic of the presentation in advance of the interview. You can then devote enough time to thinking about the title you have been given in order to prepare for the day. Even if you have not been given the topic in advance you need not panic. You will normally be allocated a certain amount of preparation time on the day, often up to an hour, in order to collect your thoughts and ideas to present to the interview panel. It is rare for the topic to be completely unexpected. It is likely to be concerned with some aspect of the job and time spent thinking about, and planning for, possible topics for the presentation will be well spent.

Types of presentation

Here are 10 examples of different presentation topics that could be set. These presentation topics range in difficulty depending on the job applied for. In each case though, you would need to think what you want to put forward as your main key points:

1. Prepare a five-minute outline of your ideas for developing this position.

2. Have ready a 15-minute presentation on one of your priorities in this role.

3. We would like you to talk for 10 minutes on the key issues that you think are facing this organisation.

4. Please have ready a 10-minute outline of your main work achievements to date.

5. Tell us in five minutes or less why we should give you this job.

6. Explain to us in 15 minutes how you see the main strengths, weaknesses, opportunities and threats facing this company.

7. Please tell us about an instance where you have managed change.

8. We want to move to a more customer-focused culture. What advice would you give us?

9. What would you recommend to help us survive this economic downturn?

10. Present to us in 20 minutes how you would take this department forward.

Sometimes you will be asked to present different sorts of material. Exercises may be set where you have to evaluate material and then present your decisions to the panel, either in writing or in person.

Exercises can include simulations of aspects of the job you are applying for, for example, an in-tray exercise for a senior administrative position. Here you could be asked to read various documents as if they were in an in-tray awaiting your views, decisions and actions. One letter may be about a problem that has arisen between members of staff; another e-mail may cover the need for a group meeting on a strategic matter where you need to take a lead by setting the agenda, and another document may be asking for your views on a technical problem. You will be judged on your ability to prioritise, make decisions and manage varied situations according to the way you deal with and respond to the documents in this simulation. Knowing the organisation concerned and feeling clear about the priorities that exist there will help you tackle this kind of activity. For instance, in an in-tray exercise of the kind described above, think through which element you would give priority to.

Another kind of presentation is being involved in a discussion. Discussions are often used for jobs or courses involving a high level of people-skills. They may take place with other candidates, sometimes with other staff, sometimes both together. An example of this kind of approach is with some senior Civil Service appointments where candidates are asked to give advice on a topical subject to someone acting in the role of the Government Minister in whose department the job is located.

You could be given topics to debate under observation and will often be assessed on your ability to work with the group rather than just how you convey your own opinions. This means that helping others to join in and encouraging full and open debate could be more important than winning all the arguments. If you may face this kind of activity, you need to have thought through your tactics in advance. For instance, in a sales environment, your ability to 'tune in' to others, tailor your conversation to theirs and reach mutual agreement might be impressive, whereas for a political researcher's job, thorough and detailed analysis and drawing firm conclusions may point to success.

Case study

One national organisation makes all candidates for management positions give a presentation. However, this presentation is not in front of the interview panel. Instead it is given to the very team of staff that the candidate will be managing if they are successful. The subject of the presentation is 'why I want this job and how I would do it'. The team of staff are afterwards asked for their perceptions of the strengths and weaknesses of each presentation. The subsequent panel interview makes the final choice of candidate but the team's feedback is always taken into account. The most successful candidates concentrate on describing their management style and approach to working with teams in general terms rather than trying to second-guess exactly what the wider team is currently working on.

Preparing a presentation

You need to prepare for giving a presentation even more fully than you would for just a straightforward interview. First spend time thinking about the question if you have been set it in advance: talk it through with others, write yourself notes and mull it all over in your mind. If you do not have the topic, and it will be provided only on the day of the interview, you can still do some valuable preparation. What kind of question might they set for you? It could be one that is similar to the examples above on pages 73–74. Are there any particular aspects of the job that they might want to hear about? Is the organisation going through any kind of change or challenge at the present time? What do you think are the most significant parts of the job and how would you handle them? You need to be ready to talk on any of these points on the day.

Once you have some initial ideas, try to structure your session into three key points so that it is easy to follow. Do not try to pack too much information in, as a few clear points are better than a lot of confused material.

Here is an example of planning for a presentation on topic number 4 (page 73) 'Your main work achievements to date'; you might decide to have as your three key points:

1. my main achievements at work;

2. my specific role in these achievements;

3. what characteristics I demonstrated.

For topic number 5 (page 73) 'Why should we give you this job?' you could decide to include:

1. my skills and experience;

2. my personality;

3. how I can contribute to the future of this organisation.

It does not really matter what your three key points are; this structure just allows you to group your thoughts and organise your material so that it can easily be followed by your audience. Always start with an introduction and explain what you are going to be talking about in your presentation. Finish with a summary of the key points that you have made and invite questions if that is appropriate. Don't try to be funny, quirky or dramatic in your presentation. Members of the panel have probably seen it all before and may not share your sense of humour. You are much more likely to impress them by being clear, direct and well-organised in what you are saying.

Rehearsing your presentation

No actor goes on stage without proper rehearsals, the final one in full dress. You should do the same. Practise what you want to say out loud to get yourself used to the key points. Practise in front of:

■ a mirror, so that you know how you are going to look;

■ friends, so that you can check that what you are saying makes sense;

■ the clock, so that you can time your presentation accurately. You must stick to the time limit you have been given. Interviewers will often just cut you off if you over-run, which could ruin your presentation entirely. Many presentations go on for too long – make sure yours is not one of them.

Projecting yourself

Delivering a presentation requires a bit more energy than the normal interview because you will be giving a performance. Always give your presentation standing up if you get the chance. It is easier for people to concentrate on what you are saying if they can see you clearly. You need to present your material in a slightly larger than life manner with broader gestures, more projection and variety in your voice and greater animation than you might normally use. If you think your nerves might stop you performing in this way, you need to think of it as a show that you are putting on for the audience. You will mainly be asked to make a presentation if the job concerned means you will often be in this position. Think about the way that you would give group presentations if you were doing the job and this may help you on the day – you can imagine yourself to be in the post already.

Using visual aids

You may be offered computer facilities, flip charts or other visual aids to use in your presentation. Think very carefully before using a programme such as Microsoft PowerPoint to provide a series of screens to accompany your talk. Unless you are dealing with a large audience or need to put across complex material, it will normally do you no favours to use this kind of presentation software. In a short presentation, a simple handout of your main points will be enough of a visual back-up to enhance your presentation and PowerPoint can also be helpful for producing these.

Do not try to use anything that you are not confident or comfortable with. When you are under stress, it is not the best time to experiment with unfamiliar bits of equipment or technology. Apart from the technical difficulties, you should resist the temptation to duplicate everything you are saying on PowerPoint or you will bore your audience. Any visual back-up you use should be to add interest to what you are saying and to reinforce your main points. Use pictures where possible rather than words and avoid figures and statistics. Charts and graphs, if clearly displayed, can be an effective way of getting across complex information. There are aston-ishing amounts of images available including pictures, cartoons and symbols. Look at Clip Art on your computer – copyright free images you can use as you like in any presen-tation. Don't be tempted to get too ambitious – keep your graphics simple so that they add to your presentation, not detract from it. Let your message do the talking, not the tech-nology.

You should ask yourself: Who is this presentation to? How will using presentation software add to my impact? If you are presenting to a large group, then using software to show where you are going with your presentation may be useful. PowerPoint can also be useful if you need to show visually some complicated relationship – such as a downturn in the economy. One graph can put over the facts much more simply than hearing reams of detailed statistics.

A senior government employee who conducts frequent interviews told me:

'We always ask for presentations and I dread people who come in and plug in the laptop. It is bound to be a tedious presentation where everything they show me, they have already told me. All I want to know is that they can stand up and deliver a sensible presentation; I do not want to see endless and pointless graphics on a screen which duplicate everything and add nothing. If they can't speak engagingly to me unaided, then using PowerPoint certainly won't help them to get the job.'

Dos and don'ts

✔ Do keep it simple and direct.

✔ Do summarise your presentation in a hand-out or *aide-mémoire* for the panel to keep afterwards (make sure your name is on it).

✔ Do enjoy the presentation when you give it, to show you like this element of the work.

✗ Don't pitch it too high; you may go over the heads of everyone present.

✗ Don't talk in a different language to normal; avoid jargon and initials.

✗ Don't try to pack too much information into a short presentation; less is more.

Points to remember

1. Good presentations do not happen by accident, they have to be worked on.

2. The impression you want the employer to have is that you are the candidate with the most to offer and who is full of good ideas.

3. Structuring your presentation clearly will help the audience understand it.

4. Try to include some visual element to get your points across.

5. The delivery of your presentation needs as much work as the content. Practice makes perfect.

Answering interview questions

Examples of interview questions and answers

The longest part of any job interview tends to be the time devoted to questions asked of the candidate. It is also the cause of most stress for candidates. We worry whether we will be able to answer the questions convincingly; whether anything will come up to catch us out and if our answers are as impressive as those of the other candidates. It is the case that the more we know in advance about the questions to be asked, the more comprehensive our preparation and the more confident our delivery on the day. Whilst it is impossible to accurately predict every single question that will be asked in an interview, we can guess fairly accurately most of the likely areas to be covered.

Think about the questions from the employer's point of view. He or she only has a limited time to come to a decision about which is the best candidate from those on the shortlist. If all candidates are to be asked the same or similar questions so that their answers can be compared and contrasted together, there needs to be a list of questions prepared and ready to ask in advance of the interview. If a job description and personnel specification exist for the post, these will form the basis of a lot of the questioning. If the employer has taken the trouble to be explicit in advance about what will be done in the job and the essential and desirable qualities required for the job, these lists provide a predictable direction for questioning in the interview.

The employer is likely to start with questions that explore the backgrounds of the candidates, frequently covering education, training and experience. Most interviewers like to ask about any interests or hobbies that the candidates may have, to find out what kind of person they are outside, as well as inside, the workplace. More general questions will follow about attitudes, aptitudes and abilities plus perhaps some exploration of any ideas the candidates have about how they would approach carrying out the job on offer. For more senior or specialised roles, there may well be some questions designed to see if the candidates have a vision of how they would develop the role, if appointed.

Here is a selection of typical questions that you may be asked in an interview. Following each question are some suggestions about the type of information that the interviewer would be interested in as part of your answer. You will rarely be asked *all* these questions, and some may not apply to you, but as full a range as possible has been included to give you practice at how to respond. If you can answer all these 50 questions confidently you are truly ready for your interview. Read each question, then covering up my guidelines underneath, try to answer as if you were in an interview. Then read my comments and see if there is anything you would subsequently alter about the answer you gave.

You will see that a full answer for each question has been suggested. You are only being asked these questions to prompt you to talk about yourself. The more information you can give, the more helpful it will be, so long as your answers are concise, clear and relevant. Giving lots of detail is not as important as stressing what skills you have used or experience you have gained.

Many people feel that they should not repeat information that they have already given on their CV or application form for fear of sounding repetitive and boring to the interviewer. This is a mistaken view. Any paper application that you made would have been considered along with those of several, if not many, other people. Your paperwork may have been read in a hurry, sometimes a long time ago and not been looked at since. It is unlikely that much will be remembered and even if it is, it does not hurt to reiterate how good a candidate for this vacancy you really are. Shortlisting for the post may have been carried out by a member of the HR team who may not even be on the panel. The actual interviewers may know nothing about your background at all, so do not worry about repeating information already in your application.

Education and training

Q1. 'Why did you decide to go to college?'

This requires a full answer, and you need to go back to when you left school in order to be able to answer it. What were your long-term ambitions at the time? Were there certain subjects you particularly enjoyed at school and wished to continue to study? How and why did you choose your particular course and your specialist subjects?

Perhaps you studied as a mature student. What factors led to your decision to return to learning in this way? The employer will be interested in your motivation. It is important to show that you did not just drift into attending college on the academic conveyor belt but that you made your own clear choices along the way.

Q2. 'Can you tell me about your college course?'

This kind of open question about any education or training you have completed invites you to make connections that can impress your interviewer. For instance, were there any aspects of your college course that could have a direct bearing on the job for which you are being interviewed? Do you feel that you learned more from one part of the course than another? Were there any extra-mural or external activities that you took part in that now have any relevance to this vacancy?

Many people forget to explain exactly where they went to college and precisely which course they took. Even if the employer already has this information on your CV or application form, he or she may not have it to hand, or even remember having seen it before. What sort of teaching methods were employed? Were there compulsory core modules or subjects and specialist options? How did you decide which to study?

Q3. 'Did you enjoy any particular part of your studies more than the rest?'

This question gives you the chance to show some enthusiasm. Bring up in your response all those things that you found stimulating and rewarding about your course. This is a chance to show how positive you can be about good things you have experienced. Even if you struggled through college, dropped out of the course early or did less well than you expected, there must be some aspect of the experience that you can discuss here. Try to find an example that links with the job you are applying for. Perhaps if you were being interviewed for a sales vacancy you could say: 'In my second year and above we were asked to talk to potential students each year. I enjoyed explaining the course to them, answering their questions and giving them advice about their application. I felt like an ambassador for the college at those times.'

The employer is trying to find out what sort of person you are to get clues about the sort of work that would suit you best. Was there some particular module or course that you enjoyed more than others? Did it involve working alone or with other people?

Think about the impression you will create with particular answers. Talking at length about how much you enjoyed researching alone for hours in the chemistry laboratory at college will indicate your preferred style of working. The interviewer will probably assume that you are not the team player that he or she is looking for.

Q4. 'Can you tell me about a project that you worked on at school or college?'

Working life is full of dealing with projects of one kind or another, from getting a document sent, to managing a building contract, to supervising a team of accounts clerks. This question is being asked because the answer will give an indication of the way you would deal with this kind of work. You will need to explain how the project was conceived, what the task was, who else was involved in the work, how you worked together, how you handled any difficulties, your particular contribution and what you think you gained from the exercise, particularly if you learned anything.

Were there any particular issues in the management of the project that were significant? What helped or hindered at the planning stage? Did everything go according to plan? Looking back, what would you do differently?

Q5. 'Would you recommend your course to other people and, if so, why?'

The interviewer will want to hear that you are positive about college overall otherwise it might give the impression that you are a person who makes choices that are not good for you, but you can be fairly balanced in your answer to a question like this. Try to say both what you thought were the strengths of the course and what people might not like about it. How would you rate the quality of the teaching you received? What about the overall experience of being at your college? Did your fellow students feel the same way as you about the course? If you were talking to prospective students today, can you think of a way that you could summarise your whole experience at college? Is there anything that you know now about your course that you wish you had known when you began your studies? Most employers want to recruit people who are keen to keep up with their learning, so enthusiasm for your studies will earn you extra points here.

Q6.   'What do you feel you gained from going to college?'

This question could be asked of a recent college leaver. It gives you a chance to summarise your personal growth whilst a student. Looking back at yourself when you first went to college compared to how you are now, how do you think you changed? How have you grown in understanding, both of your subjects studied but also in your knowledge of working with other people? Do you feel different now that you are a graduate? The employer will be interested to see how mature you are in terms of what you choose to include in your answer to this question. Don't focus too heavily on the social side of life, even if that is where you feel you really gained most. Describe the parts of your studies that enhanced your knowledge and see if you can include the need for discipline when studying and growing into taking responsibility for yourself whilst at college.

Employment history

Q7.   'Have you had any work experience?'

This question is often asked of younger people who have just left full-time education. No employer wants to hear that you are completely inexperienced, even if you only left college a week ago. If you took part in any practical placements at college, talk about them here. You will need to come up with some kind of answer in order to reassure the interviewer that you are used to the routine of work, that you can hold down a position and that someone else has wanted to employ you in the past. Perhaps you have done a paper round; worked on voluntary projects while at school; had holiday or vacation jobs or participated in a work experience programme at school or college.

If you have never done any type of work at all, do not let this situation continue as now is the time to start. You could offer your services to a community organisation on a voluntary basis or 'work shadow' some friend or relative who does what you are interested in. A training course could help you pick up many transferable skills. If you are studying it may be possible to get a Saturday or evening job. Apart from providing you with a positive response to this question, and giving you added purpose and contacts, the work experience may enable you to gain a character reference from the organisation concerned. Voluntary or temporary work can also show you whether you would like a certain job or not by giving you a trial period to see what it involves.

Q8. 'Can you tell me about your last job?'

First you need to summarise the main features of your last job so that your interviewer can quickly and easily understand what you were doing, why and how. Forget that you have already written about this in your CV or application form. Imagine this is the first time you have discussed the job. Think through in advance what aspects of the job will be impressive to this employer and stress how you have learned about these areas in particular. It is not the precise details of what you were doing in the job that are wanted, but an account of the main skills involved and what you contributed to the organisation. Try to include skills that will be just as useful to this new job. Explain how you carried out the main tasks. Give concrete examples where possible to illustrate your points and stress how you progressed in the course of the job.

Q9. 'What did you enjoy most in your last job?'

This question is a gift for you to show your enthusiasm for work in particular and for those elements of your last job that demonstrate your skills that are directly transferable to the new job. Think about the job on offer today and work out which elements link most directly with your last job. Talk about how you would like to take these areas further and develop your skills more fully. Show, by what you enjoyed most, what the special contribution is that you can offer the interviewer. If you are applying for a sales job, talk about the progress you made on the sales floor in your last job and how you would be keen to learn more in this area. If you are going to be working in a team in the new job, find an example of how working with others comes easily to you. If you need to be responsible for certain areas, illustrate that you enjoyed being in charge in your last role and give some examples of how this worked for you and your last employer.

Q10. 'What did you find most challenging in your last job?'

Now the interviewer does not want to hear a long list of things you struggled with. You are trying to give the impression that you are capable and positive. However, you do have to provide an answer to this question so take time to think what would be a good topic to choose. It will be best if you can find an example of some difficulty that you managed to overcome. Working in teams often throws up challenges

Have you ever sorted out a dispute between other people? Did you solve problems for clients or customers that seemed tricky to start with? Perhaps there was a lot to learn in the last job you had, that you overcame through effort and hard work? Think through a real situation that also shows you can rise to and overcome challenges when you meet them.

Q11. 'Tell us about an area in your last job where you feel you could have performed better.'

Not many of us are perfect so you will probably be able to think of some area to discuss in your answer fairly easily. Make sure that it does not show you to be a failure though. If you had a total disaster in some area of your work that stopped production for days or ruined a big project, don't bring these examples up unless you can make a lot of how you learned from the experience so that it will never happen again. The best answers will include some element of going one step back to end up two steps further on. If you found a way to shorten a process, increase the efficiency of the department or better serve your clients, then these would all be good examples to give to show you as a candidate who strives to improve.

Q12. 'Why did you leave your last position?'

This is not the time to decry either your last job, the people you worked with or the employer concerned. A candidate who appears to have difficulty in getting on with people will definitely not be offered a new position. Nobody wants to risk employing a troublemaker. You will need to provide positive reasons for moving on from your last job, either involving different work or preferably taking up a new opportunity – to study, do voluntary work, or whatever you say you have been doing since you stopped work. If there were major problems in your last (or present) job that you wish to mention, you should only talk about possible improvements which could be made in order to sound upbeat.

If you had a terrible time in your last job and feel that nothing good happened to you there, try looking back at the experience now. With hindsight you may be able to describe some learning points for you personally, aspects of your time there that did teach you about the world of work in a positive manner, or motivating factors to leave that could seem useful to the interviewer. For instance: you felt that you wanted a role with more responsibility, greater challenges or more scope to be creative. This will help you to build the impression that you will be able to give a lot more in this new job.

If you are currently employed, make sure that you do not sound desperate to escape from your job. You must provide illustrations of the way you could contribute to the position for which you have applied.

Q13. 'What have you been doing since you left your last job?'

This is a good question which you can easily use to your advantage. If you are not working, and even if you have been unemployed for some time, you must come up with something positive that you have been doing with your time since you last worked. It is not enough to say that you have been looking for another job – that will be assumed.

The best answer will be either that you have been doing some sort of course to improve your skills or that you have been doing some voluntary work. If you know someone who runs a business, it may be possible to say that you have been doing some freelance contract work, helping out with this company.

Whatever you say will need to be backed up with details of your activities if the employer wishes to know more. If you are not doing anything with your time – you must start something immediately. Apart from being an absolute necessity for your CV and job applications, it is the perfect antidote to the depression that can come with unemployment. Volunteering to help out in a local organisation can help you develop new skills, gain experience, get training, explore your career interests, increase your contacts, build your confidence and help you to make new friends. Contact your local volunteer bureau to see what opportunities are available in your area. The government website www.direct.gov.uk gives details of local opportunities for voluntary work.

Q14. 'What will your last employer say about you if we ask for a reference?'

You may get asked this question even if your last employer has already filled in a reference. The interviewer wants to know about two things: first how well you got on in the last job and second, how you think other people see you. Talk up about your strong points in your answer, particularly those that will be useful in the job for which you are being interviewed. You can include negative points as long as they don't detract from the overall positive image you are trying to create. You could say that your old boss might think that you could be quite direct in your opinions sometimes but that you know he always valued your honest feedback. Or that your old supervisor might describe you as being the life and soul of the work team but that when there was a crisis you would be the first to volunteer to help out.

Q15. 'What would your colleagues from your last job say about you if we asked them?'

This question is being asked to see how you fit into a team. How were you seen in your last job – as the joker, the quiet one, the innovator or the thinker? Describe how your colleagues would describe you at your best on a good day. You can leave out the reasons for any tensions in the group for this answer and just highlight your strengths. If there were some people with whom you did not get on, that is quite normal and you could say: 'Not everyone was my best friend of course but on the whole I was a valued and respected member of the team and we worked well together.' The interviewer just wants to know that you will not be having rows every day with your new team mates.

Q16. 'What has been your greatest achievement in your working history?'

Some hard thinking before the interview is needed in order to answer this question. The example that you choose should convey some of the principal qualities needed in the job applied for and should be explained clearly and concisely. What characteristics did you demonstrate at the time? Pick an example that has close relevance to this job to show that the skills you were using are transferable to the post on offer. A useful way to make sure you don't ramble is to structure your answer into three key points. The first point could cover what the achievement was, the second could explain the circumstances or the background and the third point could explain why you feel that this represents the greatest achievement in your work to date.

Q17. 'Can you tell me about a problem that you have had to deal with?'

The point of this question, as far as the employer is concerned, is to see how you would tackle obstacles at work. An idea answer would involve you in thinking through a difficulty and solving it with the help of other people. If you can indicate some general lessons that you learned from the experience so much the better. Please do not volunteer an answer that makes you look as though you could not deal with the problem. Make sure you choose something that shows your role to be positive, practical and ultimately successful. If you worked with other people to solve the problem, had to communicate clearly and learned something from the experience, so much the better. It could involve dealing with difficult customers, a mix-up of resources, rescuing an organisational mess, in fact anything where your role has had a major effect for the good.

Q18. 'What would you do if you had a problem that you could not deal with – perhaps if you were faced with a difficult customer?'

This question is being asked to assess your ability to handle customers and provide them with the best care you can. Everybody has to ask for help at times during their working life. Your answer should show that you would not give up as soon as you were faced with a problem, such as an irate or awkward customer. The employer wants to see that you would be responsible and calm in your dealings with customers who are important stakeholders in any business. Explain that you would try to find out the exact nature of the problem troubling the person, while calming him or her down, if necessary. You need to apologise quickly in cases like this. Apologising does not mean taking all of the blame – you can feel sorry that the customer feels upset and show empathy. It can really diffuse the tension. In many cases you would be able to sort out the problem yourself, but in particularly difficult or complex cases, sometimes the issue needs to be dealt with at a higher level.

Tell the interviewer that you are aware that if this were the case you would need all the details in order to pass them on to whoever could sort out the problem. Apologising to the customer for the delay, you would tell him or her exactly when the problem would be attended to. You would then pass on the query to your supervisor or the person responsible.

Q19. 'Which of all your jobs have you found the most interesting, and why?'

It is easy to hear a question like this and yet forget to answer the second part of the question. You need not only to have the most interesting of your jobs to talk about but also be ready to explain clearly exactly what was so interesting about it. This question may be asked if you have had a varied employment history. A wise answer would include work similar to the job on offer to show that you will be happy and involved in your work. Try to justify your choice by giving examples of your main achievements in the time spent there, or explaining the particularly interesting aspects.

Q20. 'What are the most satisfying and the most frustrating aspects of your present/last job?'

You may be asked this question to find out what you like best and least about your most recent position. Think carefully before you phrase your answer. The most satisfying aspects of the job should be those most closely linked to the position that you are now applying for. A long list of frustrations can make you sound like a moaner. If there was some particularly difficult aspect of the job, try to say how you helped to improve it. If at the time you did not, or could not rectify it, can you think of remedies now that might work? Make sure the frustrations are not also present in the job you are applying for now. This is important as you will not be offered a job if something that annoys you turns out to be a large part of the job on offer.

Interests

Q21. 'What hobbies or interests do you have?'

Why should employers be interested in the answer to this question? Is it pure nosiness? Everything you say about yourself contributes to the general impression gained about you. If I tell you that my hobbies are knitting, cookery, needlework, decorating cakes and bird-watching, you have an idea of the sort of person I am. If, however, I tell you that my hobbies include karate, African music, organising a community group, gardening and swimming, the picture is quite different.

You need to think hard about which hobbies and interests to mention. They can illustrate that you have a well-rounded personality and lead a full and satisfying life. Examples of times when you were in a leading or organising role will create a good impression.

There are some interests that we all have in common and these are not worth listing. We all read, watch television and socialise with other people, and these activities should not be part of your answer unless you have something specific to say about them. Be warned that if you mention them, you are likely to be asked either 'What was the last book you read?' or 'Can you tell me about a television programme that interested you lately?' Details of the latest episode of your favourite soap opera will not suffice!

Do not be too specific about any political or religious interests unless they are of direct relevance to the job in question. It is better just to say, as in the example above, that you are actively involved in the local community. The interviewer may hold different views from your own and what may be a passion to you may be seen as a prejudice to him or her.

You do not have to spend time on all the hobbies that you mention, but be sure that you know enough to talk about the subject in some depth. Employers often pick on hobbies as an easy area of questioning and will be interested in discussing more unusual choices.

You should have some knowledge of every hobby that you mention, even if you need to say: 'Well, I am very interested in windsurfing. At the moment I am finding out about it, but I intend to spend some time next summer having a go,' or 'I used to play a lot of basketball at school. I'm a bit rusty now, but I watch it when I can and am joining an evening class shortly to brush up my skills.'

The three points to be aware of when answering this question are:

■ Include a variety of interests – some using your mind and some sporting or physical activities to show that you are a lively, healthy and active person. Try to have at least one practical interest and one which uses your mental aptitudes. Include some group activities and some you do on your own.

■ Ensure that you have at least one pastime which is different from other people's and is unusual or will provoke discussion. This makes it easier for employers to ask you follow-up questions and to remember you subsequently.

■ Be prepared to discuss any of the topics you mention in some detail.

Q22. 'Tell me about your favourite activity outside work.'

For your answer to this question, which is a more specific version of question 21, you can just concentrate on what you like doing best. What really fires up your enthusiasm? How do you like to spend your time after work? The activity you pick has to be something other than watching TV unless you watch a specific type of programme on TV such as history programmes or wildlife documentaries that you can talk about in some detail. Seeing friends is something that we all do, unless you go hill walking with yours or plan regular holidays together, in which case it will do fine. The stress should be on the activity, ie something in which you are actively involved.

Please don't be tempted to make up an exotic hobby for this question or you may find that the interviewer, to whom you have just bluffed about being a karate expert, has a black belt in that sport herself. You would find it impossible to continue making things up if you were sitting across from an expert in that subject and it could lose you your chance of the job. It is better to talk about something real that you enjoy a lot, even if it is not very exciting. Let your enthusiasm for the activity do the talking.

General

Q23. 'What are your strengths?'

This is one of my favourite questions. If you were ever given a chance to shine – this is it. Although at first sight this seems daunting, it is easy to prepare an impressive answer if you consider it before the interview.

In the space below make a list of 10 of your good qualities. Each point should comprise one word or short phrase and should relate to your behaviour at work.

Examples could be: 'Flexible; good at keeping to deadlines; calm; can work under pressure ...' Everybody's list will be different. If you find this exercise difficult, try to imagine what your mother, your best friend, your dog – or whoever loves you most in the world – would say about you if they were describing your best characteristics to a stranger.

YOUR 10 STRENGTHS

1. _____
2. _____
3. _____
4. _____
5. _____
6. _____
7. _____
8. _____
9. _____
10. _____

Once written down, this list is very useful as the basis for answering any question about your strengths. By selecting five or six points from your list, you can put together a clear and powerful answer. Because you have prepared in advance, you will sound confident about your own abilities and proud of your character.

The items on your list do not have to be in any order; just write them down as they occur to you. Do not qualify them by saying 'fairly good at …' or 'some people think I am …', just list them as you have been asked to. You do not have to prove any of them – simply outline your most impressive characteristics.

Most people find it hard to compile the list of their 10 strengths, and even harder to talk about them in an interview. Do not worry about sounding boastful. It is much more common for candidates to be too modest than to blow their own trumpets. I recommend that you don't hold back from explaining just how good you are in this answer.

The list of 10 points can be kept and added to throughout your life. Whenever a colleague or friend compliments you on some aspect of your character, add it to your list. More words of praise may come from appraisals with employers, development reviews at work or as references when you leave a job. Keep your list growing as you collect these compliments. It will prove useful when you need to write about your personality for a CV, describe your strengths for an application form or prepare for future interviews. It also provides a welcome confidence boost when needed, instantly recalling your talents when you are at your brilliant best.

Q24. 'What are your weaknesses?'

Whatever does the employer mean by asking this question? Nobody will want to employ someone who can reel off a long list of serious faults. The best way to answer is not to admit to any weaknesses at all. An example could be: 'At my age I know myself pretty well and don't think I have any major weaknesses.' If you do mention weaknesses, make sure that they are those which sound more like strengths. For instance: 'I sometimes take my work too seriously and will stay late at the office to get something finished,' or 'I tend to be very flexible as a work colleague, and I will do the jobs that no one else wants to do.' No employer will mind you having weaknesses like these.

Q25. 'What are you most proud of?'

This should normally relate to some experience at work, and it is helpful if it can demonstrate the necessary qualities for the job on offer. Any project or team work where you played a significant role could be mentioned. Any instance where your contribution made a real difference, where you tried an innovative approach or learned something new would be well worth mentioning. The interviewer does not want to hear about examples where you gained personally but rather when you made a positive impact on a previous employer.

Here are some examples:

- overcoming a persistent problem;

- a time when you did really well;

- when you added value for the employer, customers or clients;

- when you worked with a team to reach or beat targets;

- when you helped the organisation to develop or grow.

Q26. 'Which current affairs problem have you been aware of lately?'

This is a favourite question for public service jobs and is designed to check two things. The first is that your understanding of the world is wide and up to date, and the second is to see what sort of political attitudes you have. It therefore makes sense to read a quality daily newspaper thoroughly for at least a week before any interview. This is particularly relevant when you have applied for a job where you would be representing the views of the employing organisation to other agencies or clients.

Employers rarely want candidates to express strong political views in interviews. This is certainly true of the Civil Service, not-for-profit sector and local authorities. Ideally, you should illustrate that you know about a current issue in some depth, you are aware of the two sides to the argument, you can understand the feelings on both sides, and you realise what a difficult political problem it is.

Politics should be left to politicians, or to any of us in our private lives, not brought into the workplace. If you are asked for your opinion on a political issue, refrain from coming down heavily on either side. Government or local authority employers want to be sure that you are aware of the need to put into practice the wishes of the political leaders of the day – and they can be right or left wing.

Q27. 'What do you see yourself doing in five years' time?'

This is a similar question to one about your career ambitions. Think – why is the employer asking this? Does he or she want to know that you plan to train as an accountant or an actor in your spare time, and leave this job as soon as possible? No. He or she wants a member of staff who is serious about this particular vacancy and interested in staying put for a considerable time. Your answer could indicate that you hope to be in the company, but perhaps with greater responsibilities. Not everyone is seeking promotion. You could say that you would be interested in gaining a more specialist role.

Q28. 'Why should we employ you rather than another candidate?'

This is another good question as it enables you to use your list of 10 strengths again. (See question 23 above.) Employers are interested in hearing about your skills, experience and personality.

In your answer you could mention any of your particular skills which relate to the job, your relevant experience, and add those aspects of your personality which best suit you for the position. A question like this is a gift to an interviewee. Do not be worried about boasting. This is the time to 'sell yourself' strongly to the interviewer. You are being asked to summarise your application – and the answer to this question is the crux of the whole interview. Getting the job may depend on your answer so it has to be impressive.

You can bring in your ideas here – explain the thoughts you have had about the organisation and your vision for the future of the job. The more senior the position that you are applying for, the more likely it is that no one on the panel knows exactly what they are looking for when recruiting. By definition, the more rare or specialised the role, the fewer people there will be who fully understand how the job could or should be done. In addition, the more significant the position for the organisation, the more important it will be to have it filled by someone with ideas and initiative. You can show that you will bring added value to the job in comparison with the other candidates by sharing your view of the way the job should be carried out. This requires you to have spent some serious thinking time considering the job, the situation of the organisation and the possibilities of the role.

Q29. 'What other careers are you interested in?'

If you are applying for a computer operator's job in order to pay the rent and secretly want to be a police officer or a ballet dancer, keep that to yourself. Again, think – why is the employer interested in this question? He or she will be most impressed by the candidate who seems serious about the job on offer and about making a career in this line of work. Talk more about your interest in this work. What attracted you to apply and why do you think you are suitable for it? Imply that your career ambitions are in this exact field. You could add that in the future you would be interested in working your way up to a position with more responsibility, or perhaps specialising in a particular area of the work.

Q30. 'Which other organisations have you applied to work for?'

This question has similarities to the one above. The employer does not want a candidate whom every other company has rejected. They feel their organisation is special and offering you the job represents a big investment. You want to convey the impression that you feel this particular vacancy is exactly the right one for you, and you have been saving yourself for it. I recommend that you say you are being choosy about the companies you approach. In other words, imply that you have not found such an interesting vacancy as this before, and say why.

Q31. 'What does equal opportunities mean to you?'

This is the most difficult question to answer and one people worry about. But, fortunately, most interviewers themselves are not too sure what the correct answer is. Think this through. Why would the employer be asking this question? The employer must be concerned with offering services or goods to the widest range of the public. They only want employees who share their interest in providing fairly and equitably to their users, clients or customers. As long as you demonstrate that you understand the importance of everyone getting the same chances in employment and access to services, the employer will be impressed.

Many people answer: 'Treating everyone in the same way.' I think this answer is a little too simple. Some people with special needs may need extra help. For instance, someone with a visual impairment may need special facilities or aids in order to do their job properly. You may have some personal awareness of this subject and feel like expressing it in the interview. For instance: 'As a woman, I know how it feels not to be taken seriously sometimes, so I always try to make sure that I treat everyone with respect,' or 'When I first arrived in this country I felt like an outsider and I am keen to help those who may need more support to make full use of the services offered by this organisation.'

Q32. 'How would you put equal opportunities into practice?'

This is often asked together with the previous question. The trick here is to think about the best answer in the light of the organisation applied to. Why has the employer decided to ask you this? It is likely that the current vacancy is with a large organisation, not-for-profit organisation or local authority which is looking for staff who will be aware of two things: first, that services need to be made available to the whole population and, second, that colleagues may need support and understanding too. Explain how you would aim to fulfil these requirements in that job both internally and externally.

Draw on past experience and think of practical steps that can be taken to achieve this, such as translations of documents into different languages or by using visual images that are representative of the client group.

Q33. 'When have you needed to be at your most tactful in your work?'

A question asking for unusual examples of behaviour can take us by surprise, so it is good to plan for a curve-ball question like this that can come out of the blue. The interviewer will be interested to see what kind of answer you come up with and will be able to gauge if exhibiting tactful behaviour is something that you do regularly. It may be a very relevant question if your new team is full of prickly characters but probably means that the new job involves dealing with clients, colleagues or customers who will respond to you being tactful. Perhaps you have had experience of answering customers' queries about what suits them in the past or have had to give advice to people that they did not want to hear. Try to think about work situations where you were able to convey sensitive information smoothly and easily. Have you ever had to give feedback to people working for you or to those in your team? Have you smoothed over awkward incidents between colleagues to keep the peace? Any of these examples would be good to include in your answer.

Q34. 'What sort of person are you?'

This is a question that is wide open for you to sell yourself. Think about your strengths rather than your weaknesses. The list you compiled in question 23 can provide the basis for your answer. Try to think of the way you come over to other people in the work situation and describe yourself at your best. How would the people you got on best with in your last job talk about you? What would they say impressed them about you and what aspects of you do they miss now that you have moved on?

Q35. 'How would you describe your team/management style?'

If the job you are applying for is in management, you may well be asked how you see your management style. If not in management you could still be asked what kind of a team player you are. This question invites you to analyse yourself in terms of the way that you work with other people. Do you lead from the front? How do you convince people to do what you want them to? What would be your approach to dealing with problems in your team? If you are applying for management jobs, read some current books on being a leader to see where you fit in the range of styles described. Most people would say they consult with their team when it comes to gathering views but that sometimes they may need to make decisions that not everyone agrees with. Most of us would like to come over as firm but fair in our dealings with others. Even if you have not had much experience in managing other people, consider team experiences that you have had, to see what role you played. What makes you think you could be a good manager? Think about the best people who have managed you. What style of management would you say they exhibited?

Q36. 'Are you a creative person?'

Creativity is greatly prized in the workplace. Someone who can help to think of new ideas, or improve processes and re-assess the old ways of doing things, can be worth their weight in gold. There are not many employers who wouldn't like to employ creative people given the chance. Giving an example of being creative in the workplace will give you an advantage. Even if you cannot think of a work example, most of us can think of some way in which we demonstrate creative aspects of our character. Whether you can make things, play an instrument, grow things, cook or are artistic, you should be able to find some area to talk about if you are asked this question. It could be playing a sport or helping your children with their homework but you must come up with something. Have you been creative in the past? Enjoyed art when you were younger, visited galleries or the cinema? Find a way to be able to answer with a positive response.

Q37. 'What would you say has been your biggest mistake?'

Choose your biggest mistake carefully when answering this question. Pick an example when you were able to retrieve the situation and turn the result around. We all make mistakes but you need to cite one that turned out well or at least provided you with a valuable learning experience. If you can prove that you turned the situation around, so much the better. One good example I heard was when a team lost a contract for highly profitable work because they missed the deadline for bidding for the contract. They learned a lesson, established a much tighter checking process on dates and work plans… and managed to win the contract back again the next time it was on offer. Every team in the unit benefited from the original mistake because they all used the new system and were more effective as a result.

Q38. 'Have you made any career choices that you now regret?'

Even if you don't feel regretful about your career path to date, you can probably think of a time when you did not grab an opportunity that could have been better for you. Many of us stumble into our first job when perhaps we could have been more selective. It is best not to reveal that you secretly hanker after a major career change when you answer this question. The interviewer wants to feel that you are the perfect candidate for the job on offer, so anything that you can say to show that your career dreams have always been pointing in this direction, the better. Perhaps you struggled with some subjects at school or college and you might have been better off studying something that appealed to you more. You may feel that you stayed in earlier dead-end jobs too long rather than searching for a better opportunity. Try to re-evaluate your work decisions to see if you can come up with something that shows you are where you want to be right now but that you could have got there more directly had you made different choices.

The vacancy

Q39. 'Tell me what you know about this organisation.'

There is no excuse for not having a response to this question as it often comes up. Whatever the particular job that you are applying for, the interviewer will expect you to have some knowledge of the organisation, and the more the better.

Whether you have seen an advertisement, been sent a job description or person specification or read literature about the company, you should have some information to offer. Even if you do not really know much about the organisation and it is one of many that you are applying for, you need to remember that the employer concerned thinks the job and the organisation are unique. The more you know, the more suitable you will seem.

Make some effort to search the internet for any information that may exist. First look up the name of the organisation using a search engine. Most medium to large organisations now have a website which outlines their main business and gives details of current priorities and past endeavours. If you can find nothing on the company directly, try looking up a competitor or reading about the sector in which the company is based. If you do not have your own computer, try the local library. They will have helpful and knowledgeable staff who will help you, and many reference materials, printed and computerised, that they can introduce you to. Try to evaluate the information you research – can you draw any conclusions about the organisation from the way it is presented?

If you have found no prior information then at least use your eyes and ears in the interview. Are there brochures or posters in evidence? How do the staff seem to relate to each other and outsiders? What first impressions have you gained? Get talking to reception staff about how they find working there. Sharing your thoughts on these topics, always stressing positive points, will show you are alert and interested.

I once interviewed someone who had arrived for her appointment knowing nothing about the organisation. She had been sent no information when applying for the post but spent her time wisely once she arrived. When I asked her this same question she replied:

'Well, I saw that the walls of the main corridor are covered with thank-you letters from your clients so I know that you offer a good service to them. The waiting area is clean and tidy, which means you care about the impression you are making. I can see that the centre is full so you must be successful and your receptionist, Janice, was very friendly to me when I arrived so I know your staff like working here. When I came in I picked up your annual report and can see the variety of work you carry out with local people, which is very impressive.'

So was she and, needless to say, she got the job.

Q40. 'Why do you want to work for this company?'

Answering this question depends on the type of work offered and how much you know about the company concerned. You need to stress the particular type of organisation in relation to your own skills, strengths and personality. Your ideas about what you would do if offered the job are worth contributing here. Try to make the case for a good match between the company's aims and outlook and your own. Enthusiasm for what you can *offer* will be much more impressive than what you hope to gain by getting the position. Try to give the impression that your career so far has been leading you to this point today.

Q41. 'If you were offered this job, how do you think you would spend your first two weeks with the company?'

This is a more general question designed to check that you have a realistic and sensible approach to work. In most jobs, unless you have worked for the organisation before, you would need to spend your first few days getting used to the new environment. This means finding your way around, meeting your new colleagues, and familiarising yourself with the rules and working practices. You would also probably spend some time with your new manager learning how the work is done and about current priorities.

Q42. 'What do you think are the most important issues facing this organisation at the moment?'

This question may well be posed when certain political, environmental or financial issues affect an organisation. Examples of such organisations could be charities, not-for-profit organisations or local authorities. Your answer would depend on the exact nature of the employer, but could include: generating income; allocating scarce resources; setting objectives; implementing cutbacks; quality control; managing grant-funding or some particular campaign with which the organisation is involved. You will really have to do your homework though in order to answer this convincingly. Can you find out what the press profile of the organisation has been lately? Visit a website such as www.guardian.co.uk and search for recent news about them. That may tell you about their priorities and concerns.

Q43. 'What do you think you can contribute to this company?'

This is one of my favourite questions. As far as an employer is concerned, this represents the crux of the whole interview. This is your chance to shine, by saying exactly why you decided to apply for the job. You will need to bring out your particular strengths and show clearly what you can offer *not* what you want to get from the job. Quoting your experience and skills will help to impress on the employer that you will be a valuable addition to the team. Don't forget to include good points about your personality here. Move on to explain how you would use all these things to help build on the success of the organisation.

Take care not to appear arrogant. Even if you can see weaknesses in some of the present activities or direction of the organisation, you should only convey these in terms of what could be improved. You need to be very aware of your audience. The Marketing Director of a large company asked a candidate at an interview to comment on the latest marketing campaign. The candidate effectively ruled herself out of the job when she answered that she thought the work had been complete rubbish from start to finish. None of us responds well to negative criticism, whereas constructive and creative points are often well received.

Q44. 'Why are you applying for the post?'

This is another variant on the last question and should be answered in the same way. Try to structure your answers. Give three key points such as:

1. my skills and experience;

2. my character and personality;

3. my vision for this particular post.

In this way you will give a clearer response while still including everything you need to say.

Q45. 'Which areas of the job description are you weakest at and how would you compensate for this?'

The employer does not want to hear that you fall short of the requirements in many respects so evaluate which of the areas asked for is your weakest. You need to show what you have done already about boosting your skills and experience in this area and what else you can do in the future. If budgeting is the area you like least you could say: 'I know that the area I need to work hardest on is managing budgets as I have least experience here. It is also the most important area for having control over the work of the department. I recently went on a course for budgetary management which gave me more confidence in this field and I would be keen to work closely with the finance manager for the first six months to ensure that I was on top of this part of the role.' Showing self-knowledge plus an interest in learning and development is impressive.

Q46. 'This job is too highly paid isn't it?'

Sometimes you will be asked a provocative question like this, but the interviewer may think that this could be a question put to you by funding bodies or journalists if you get the job, so it is a good one to test you out on. If you are going for a high-profile job in the not-for-profit or charitable sector, you could be challenged on this point by the press or members of the public. Are you confident that the remuneration is worth what you would contribute to the job? Do you know what other people in similar roles are paid? None of us can really prove that we are worthwhile except by reference to work of similar value elsewhere. You will be expected to answer this with a robust defence of your role though. Talk up what special skills and talents you bring to the job and what ideas you have for developing your remit to make the organisation more impressive, effective or dynamic. Your next salary increase may depend on how convincing you are in your response.

Q47. 'This job needs to be filled by a motivator – tell us how you would do that.'

Getting people to do what you want can be difficult. You may be being asked this question as a result of current economic difficulties. If it is a sales-based job, how will you inspire your team to work harder and better? Have you had experience before of motivating people successfully? What did you do and why did it work? How are you seen by other people – as a leader and trail-blazer? Or as a safe pair of hands who can be relied on to do the right thing? How do you propose to set the expectations of your new workmates and what will you do if they do not want to work your way? Try to find examples of how you have used motivation before, or how you have been motivated by other people or circumstances in the past. Show that you are confident in this area and keen to use your skills and enthusiasm to get the team going.

Q48. 'You will have some difficult characters in your new team. How will you handle them?'

We cannot choose the people we work with so we have to find ways to get along with them. Team work is vital in any job and a good team player will always be attractive to employers. You need to draw on your past experiences whether from the work environment or outside work, to say how you would handle these new team mates who are difficult. They could be any type of people and just because they have been troublesome in the past, they could get on with you much better than they did with your predecessor. If you arrive in this organisation determined to be a productive and settled team player, that in itself could have a beneficial effect through your own behaviour helping to set a new standard for other people. You may be applying for a job where part of your role is to solve problems such as this, in which case looking at the way the individuals in the team perform in their jobs and trying to iron out any difficulties they are encountering would be a good place to start.

It may just be that you would be employed as a member of his team. Most of us respond positively to those who treat is fairly and involve us where possible so both those points hould feature in your answer. How were you treated in the ob you liked best from the past? Are there pointers there for he way that your new team should be managed? If there are insurmountable difficulties in a team in a large organisation, it might be possible to split up the team and reform the group differently. Sometimes bringing in an outside mediator to bring people together to sort out their differences can be helpful. All of these ideas are constructive and will help reassure the interviewer that you will be part of the solution to this long-running issue, not adding to the problem.

Q49. 'What do you think we should be doing to survive the economic downturn?'

Unless you are applying for a job with some kind of responsibility for strategic planning in an organisation, it is unlikely that you will be asked a question like this. However, the interviewer may want to see how you would approach answering a question about the economy or current affairs generally. There are no right answers to this question. If there were, we might not be facing difficult economic times. The interviewer will be interested to see what you think the possibilities for success are at the moment. Have you been keeping an eye on the quality press lately? Creative thinking, flexibility and diversification are three recommendations that writers in the business press are making currently. Can any of these three be applied to the job on offer? What scope is there for flair in developing new markets, ways of working or products and services? How flexible is the organisation to be able to change its ways to respond to new emerging opportunities? Can the company diversify to find new markets instead of relying on the old?

Q50. 'What do you think is the best way to deal with poor performers?'

You will be applying for a job that is concerned with the way that individuals perform at work if you are asked a question such as this. That can mean that you will work either in the

HR department or that you are a supervisor or manager of other people. Setting expectations of the way you expect people to perform at work is the place to start. Working with individuals to help them reach the standards required and investing in staff to train and develop them to the best of their abilities is crucial.

Monitoring production or performance in work is key to understanding what is happening and then giving feedback on effective working, and encouragement to motivate people can be helpful. If you have worked in this field before, describe an example of the way in which you have raised standards of performance elsewhere and show how you increased satisfaction at work. What did you do specifically to help change the situation? What are the key factors that allowed you to make the difference? Most important of all, what have you learned about staff performance that you can now bring to this new job?

Dealing with tricky situations

Starting off the interview

I recommend shaking hands with the interviewer when you enter the room; it shows that you are keen to meet him or her and able to be formally polite. Women sometimes find this difficult, as shaking hands has in the past been more of a male habit. However, because of this, it can help you both to stand out and look businesslike. Do not worry if you feel that it would be beyond your capabilities, in a nervous state, to walk in and confidently grasp a stranger's hand, but do respond positively if the interviewer wants to greet you in his way.

You will normally be invited to sit down but, if the interviewer does not mention it, do not immediately assume that he or she is playing some fiendish trick to see how you react under pressure. The much more likely explanation is that he or she has simply forgotten to invite you to be seated, in their concern about which question to ask you first. The solution is to smile and ask politely: 'May I sit down?'

Good manners

On the subject of politeness, you can never be too polite in interviews. On leaving I recommend saying: 'Thank you very much for your time. I have enjoyed meeting you. Goodbye.' Even if you are a habitual smoker, resist the temptation at the interview, if the opportunity arises. Falling ash and smoke surrounding the interviewee never look impressive, even if the employer is smoking.

Some people feel that if they are offered tea or coffee, it is impolite to refuse. But it is best *not* to accept. In my personal experience, nervousness only leads to disasters such as the cup falling on the floor or the drink filling the saucer or splashing on your interview suit. Don't be tempted to consume too much coffee beforehand either: the mixture of caffeine and adrenalin can take you way over the top. Have a strong cup of coffee after the interview is safely over.

If you do not understand or hear a question properly, do not panic. Just ask the questioner to repeat the question. It is better to do this than guess at what was said and make a mistake.

The interview does not go as planned

If you have planned your responses but do not have the chance to get your points across, you can sometimes hijack the interview so that it goes more in your favour. Suppose that you had not been asked about your strengths, and want to bring in some of the points from your list of 10 character istics from page 98. At the end of the interview you could say: 'I would just like to add a brief comment about the sort of person I am' and then say your piece.

Panic sets in

Even the most well-prepared candidate can suffer from temporary drying-up in mid-interview. If your mind goes blank, breathe deeply and play for time by saying something like: 'That's an interesting question.' You can always repeat the question to them too. This allows you a few extra seconds to collect your thoughts. If you are really stuck, ask if you could return to that question later in the interview. Similarly, if you dry up mid-answer, the situation can be retrieved. Just say, 'I'm sorry, I've just lost the thread for a minute. Could you repeat the question please?'

Don't know the answer?

Occasionally, you may be faced with a question that is just too difficult. If you cannot think of anything to say on a subject, explain so simply and without being embarrassed. If possible, indicate that it is an area you are keen to explore and learn more about in the future. Afterwards, do not let it worry you, but move on to the next question, clear that you are doing the best you can. Whatever happens, do not let this wreck your confidence.

Interviewer seems uninterested

Sometimes you can meet an interviewer who seems switched off or bored as soon as you start talking. This is very unprofessional behaviour on their part and you should not let it put you off. Keep to your planned answers and try to make eye contact as much as possible. Many interviewers lack skills in this area; they can be unconfident and uncomfortable when interviewing. Do not assume it means bad news for your prospects. He or she may just be tired, under strain or just always have that expression on their face! Carry on, do your best and do not let them put you off.

Internal vacancies

You may be applying for a promotion post or a new job in the organisation where you presently work. This would mean that you would be interviewed by current managers or colleagues, some of whom you may know quite well. Sometimes you can face this situation unknowingly. I once turned up for a job interview to find that they had brought in two outside experts to help them recruit. I was faced with not only my boss from my last place of employment but also my present one!

When you know members of the panel, they also know you. This means they may already have a view of your strengths and weaknesses and they may not expect you to be as nervous as external applicants. You cannot try to second-guess all this though. Try to remember that they have only included you in the interview process because they are serious that you may be the right person for the job. Treat them as though you do not have history with them. Even if you are very conscious of the project that went wrong or the targets that were not met, these may be the last things on their minds.

You will feel more awkward about speaking up about your strengths but you must still try to do so as you will be compared to the other candidates on the day so you must speak up for yourself. A common error many internal candidates make is to underplay their strong points in the mistaken belief that the panel will already know enough about them. If your current boss is on the panel, he or she may not know about all of your past achievements. The panel will also be making an effort to judge you by your performance in the interview alone in order to be fair to all the candidates.

Be positive about the organisation too. I heard of an internal candidate who spent much of his interview moaning about how awful everything was in the organisation where he was applying for a promotion. He was not creating a very positive impression to say the least. The last question he was asked was, 'What would you do to improve your present job?' He replied with, 'Sack all managers.' As he was being interviewed by two of his present managers, this was not the wisest of responses. Needless to say he did not get the job.

Do your best. Do not tell any more people than you have to, that you are going for the job. If you are unsuccessful, get some feedback and learn what you can then move forward. Put any disappointment behind you and look to the future.

Money

Most jobs give some indication of the salary or wages in the advertisement or job details. If money is not mentioned, avoid discussing the subject at the interview. You will obviously not take any job without knowing what you are going to be paid, but you can always check on this when the interview is over. If you are offered the job, you can say: 'I'm certainly interested in the position, but haven't yet had full details about the conditions of employment. Perhaps you could tell me the salary for the job?'

Having to negotiate your own salary

Some jobs, particularly in sales, do not have a fixed salary to offer. They set pay individually as a result of a negotiation with the candidate after a job offer has been made. You will normally know if this is the case as there will be no salary details available on advert or job details. Being forewarned means that you can think through your position prior to having to discuss it.

Start by working out exactly how much you need to earn. What is the lowest salary that you can afford to earn and still survive and maintain the lowest standard of living that you are prepared to accept?

Next what is the maximum that you could expect? Look carefully at the equivalent salaries available to see what the range covers. These two totals represent your lower and upper limits within which you can negotiate. Keep these figures to yourself, as they represent your own private calculations which should not be divulged. Any offer lower than your minimum should be rejected as impossible or unpleasant to live on. Any offer lower than your maximum amount, you should try to increase nearer to the maximum.

You may well be asked about your current pay level. Make sure you represent the whole package including any perks, overtime or bonuses that you regularly receive. Remember to calculate your present holiday entitlement as this can range between different jobs. If asked to say what salary you are expecting, you can quote the current package and say that you would want to be improving on that level. Stay enthusiastic about the job whilst in these negotiations and talk about what you think you are worth because of the contribution you can make to the role. Maintaining a position often works. When the employer is really not going to go any higher and says that it is their final offer, you need to see where such an amount comes in your limits before deciding. Remember not to be too rigid on pay though. If the job is really interesting, you may be better off accepting lower pay for better prospects in the longer run.

Dos and don'ts

✔ Do let go! Interviewers want to get to know who you are, so feel free to be yourself. Then if they don't want you for the job, that may be for the best as you may not have fitted in.

✔ Do mind the gap! Make a positive statement about things that would otherwise look negative.

✔ Do speak up for yourself – you have nothing to lose and everything to gain. Think of the interview as a kind of performance; you need to be a bit 'larger than life'.

✔ Do take care with your appearance; consider every aspect of your personal presentation.

✔ Do keep your answers simple and clear.

✔ Do speak as you would normally; there is no need to put on an act by using long words or complicated sentences.

✔ Do boast about your strengths and achievements – all the other candidates will be trying to make themselves look extra good too.

✘ Don't lose your confidence; concentrate on the vacancy that you are interested in.

✘ Don't worry about nerves – they never show to other people as much as you think they do.

✘ Don't smoke or drink tea or coffee in the interview.

✗ Don't assume that the interviewer knows what you are talking about – the things that you think are obvious may be unclear to others.

✗ Don't ever give just 'yes' or 'no' answers – the employer will want to know more than that.

✗ Don't use jargon or specialised terms without an explanation.

✗ Don't lie about yourself – you could face dismissal if you obtain a job under false pretences.

Points to remember

1. Take a minute before you answer each question to group your thoughts together clearly in your mind, as if you were giving a mini-presentation each time.

2. Try really hard to put everything relevant forward; this is your big chance.

3. Show enthusiasm where you can – everyone wants someone keen to work with.

4. Always come up with examples so you can paint a picture of what you mean.

5. If you feel you have not said all you could, ask if you can add a summary at the end.

Bringing it all together

Step-by-step checklist

Step 1. Planning

In order to feel confident you need to plan how to convince the employer that you are the best candidate for the position on the day. Get familiar with the job that you will be interviewed for. Collect any helpful information about the company. Go over your application for the post and carefully analyse the specific vacancy to understand what the employer is looking for. The successful candidate will bring out in the interview those examples of his or her background, skills and personality which complement the ones required for the position. Think about the possible challenges and opportunities of the post to give you a picture of what you would do if offered the position.

The most important point to convey is that you are the right type of person for the job. Study your list of 10 character strengths (see page 98). Select which will be the most useful at the interview. Construct sentences using the points that you have chosen, giving examples of the relevant type of behaviour. The details of previous experiences are not as important as your main achievements, the transferable skills learned or the way in which you behaved. Try to give examples where you can.

Mind the gap! Gaps can be literally breaks in your employment history or events that you need to convey in a positive light. You need to ensure that you do not sound apologetic about your experiences but can illustrate what you have learned from them. The most important thing about your answers is that they should all be positive – about your previous experience, your skills and strengths, and what makes you right for this particular job.

You can plan your journey in advance; allow extra time to ensure that you arrive at least 15 minutes early for your appointment. There is also some planning work to be done on your physical presentation. Decide which clothes to wear, concentrating on the most flattering style and colours for you. Take professional advice if necessary – a visit to an image consultant can be great fun as well as highly instructive.

Step 2. Preparation

You need to prepare yourself thoroughly for the interview. Do a dummy run of the journey to the organisation concerned if it is in an unfamiliar area. A vital part of your preparation concerns the clothes you will wear. They should all be clean, well ironed and look immaculate. Have a bath or shower and wash your hair before the interview. Give due consideration to your accessories which can contribute to the employer's important first impression of you. Keep your look plain and simple – don't clutter your appearance too much.

The most vital aspect of the preparatory stage is to speak aloud the answers that you have planned. This rehearses you for the actual performance and increases your confidence when you are asked the questions for real. Think what the interviewer is going to want to hear from you. You must sound keen and interested in the job; be someone with the right skills or be trainable, and show that you can fit into the organisation.

When you are practising your answers with a friend or in front of the mirror, be aware of how you look and sound. Your voice should be steady and clear. Try to smile while you are talking and see how it improves the way you look and sound. Rehearse your walk; holding yourself up straight can reinforce the impression of confidence as well as making it easier to breathe.

Step 3. Generating confidence

This is the time to let your enthusiasm show. One of the most attractive attributes in a job candidate is a genuine interest in the work. Do not worry about your nerves – just concentrate on enjoying the interview. You are well prepared and confident that you are the right candidate for the job, and you can look forward to meeting the employer and telling him or her about yourself.

Before the event itself, relax your face with the exercise on page 68 and take some deep breaths. Walk in with your head held up, your shoulders well back and a broad smile to make everyone present feel more at ease. The interviewers are probably quite nervous too and may not be very experienced. Shake hands if you can and remember to thank the interviewer for his or her time when you leave.

Make sure that you speak loudly and fully enough to do justice to your skills and strengths. The employer genuinely wishes to hear what you have to say and only invited you to find out about you, so do not hold back from talking about yourself and your achievements. Imagine that I am there behind you, urging you on to speak up, let your personality out and enjoy the experience. Your path to interview success starts right here. Good luck!

Step 4. Follow-up

It is wise to apply for more than one vacancy at a time, so you always have more interviews ahead of you. Be sure that each one is for a post that interests you though, otherwise you will not find the motivation to make an impressive application. This helps to keep a sense of perspective about the process and keeps you from feeling demoralised if you don't get a job. It is easy to become depressed about lack of success in job interviews. However, the most expert interviewees, even those expected to get the job, may be turned down just because, on the day, there happened to be somebody who seemed more suitable.

If you are rejected, it is worth contacting the employer to ask for some feedback on your performance in the interview. Most employers are keen to help as long as the request is phrased politely. I suggest something like:

'I have just attended an interview with you. Although I was not successful, I wondered if I could ask you for any feedback on my performance in the interview, as I am particularly interested in this type of work and your comments might help me in the future.'

Another antidote to feeling despondent about searching for work is to mix with other people in the same situation. A supportive group can keep you going when you feel at the end of your tether. At times you will need to fight the feeling that there is something wrong with you as a person. Sharing your experiences with other people will remind you that there are other excellent candidates who fail to get jobs. Maintaining some semblance of a work routine is also helpful in keeping up morale. Voluntary work, for example, provides contacts, experience, and a sense of purpose and self-worth. Some kind of study or training keeps you developing, gives you the chance to interact with others and can prove to be very rewarding.

The Government's New Deal programme may be available if you are out of work. Contact your local Jobcentre Plus to join the scheme and use their facilities, expertise and contacts. Visit www.jobcentreplus.gov.uk for more details.

If you keep getting invited to interviews then you know that your written applications are of a high standard. If you keep attending interviews, always doing your best and trying to improve, you will eventually get a job. Strongly resist feeling demoralised, depressed or unconfident. It was said earlier that interviews should be treated as learning experiences. Even if you are not successful at an interview, you can feel pleased in the knowledge that you have done your best to create a good impression.

Learning from experience

Whenever you attend an interview make a note immediately afterwards of the questions you were asked and how you replied. Try to get the wording down exactly too. Evaluate what happened. Did any of the questions take you by surprise? If so, they need fuller preparation next time. Which of your answers seemed to go down well? Why was that? Which answers would you change with hindsight? How do you feel you could have improved these answers? Could you have been more positive, spoken more fully or given more examples? If you were unsuccessful and you get feedback from the employer, endeavour to improve on your areas of weakness. You might need to get additional information, practise more or spend extra time focusing on how you fit with the next vacancy you go for. This exercise will prove very useful if you ever go for a similar vacancy, or apply to the same organisation in the future. It is also helpful to reflect on afterwards. Continuous improvement comes from looking back and learning in this way.

Other sources of help

The Connexions Service

The Connexions Service offers help and advice to young people under 19.

In some areas of the country, the staff in your local connexions service can offer help and advice to adults as well. They will have reference books about employers and applying for jobs as well as understanding and skilled staff who can help you put your CV together if you get stuck. They may also help you plan and rehearse for an important interview, or refer you somewhere which can offer this type of assistance. Find the phone number in the local phone book and ring them to find out more. For more details see www. connexions-direct.com or phone 080 800 13219.

Jobcentre Plus

Jobcentre Plus offices offer help, training opportunities and job-search resources when you are out of work. See www. jobcentreplus.gov.uk for more details.

Employment/Recruitment agencies

Agencies may help you prepare for a meeting with an employer for a particular type of job. They charge the employer if you are placed with a company.

Private career counsellors

You can get help from career counsellors who work privately and will make a charge for their service. This can be very expensive although they will help coach you for different interview situations.

Learn Direct

The Learn Direct number, 0800 101 901, is a Government-funded telephone helpline available to everyone. Ring the freephone number and you will be given advice about local sources of help on career and learning issues. This could include where to contact the types of organisations mentioned above. See www.learndirect.co.uk for more details.

Careers Advice Service

This free Government-funded service can be contacted on 0800 100 900. You can talk in confidence to a friendly, trained adviser and receive free advice on jobs, courses, paying for training or childcare.

Internet resources

Using the internet to help you with interviews

There are many internet sites that give you assistance with interview techniques. Most are sites displaying job vacancies. They make their money from recruitment advertising by employers or by taking a commission from employers if they place you in a job. As part of the information they provide around searching for jobs, these sites often include tips on interview skills and other career development issues.

Job seekers can access these pages free of charge, although if you want to use their specialised targeting process for locating the most relevant jobs to suit you, you may be required to go through a registration process. Sites run by commercial companies can charge you for CV advice or interview help. Some sites will notify you of job vacancies by e-mail or to your mobile phone.

The world wide web is a fast-changing scene and new sites appear as fast as others fall from view. Here are 10 of the current best for UK job seekers.

1. www.prospects.ac.uk
Labelled as the UK's official graduate careers website, this site is provided by Graduate Prospects, part of the Higher Education Careers Services Unit. It is aimed at graduates and provides a thorough and comprehensive guide to graduate careers and postgraduate study in the UK.

Accessible and functional, this is a useful resource for graduates and by gathering all the key points together can help to focus a graduate's job search or path to further study.

2. www.jobs.guardian.co.uk
The site is provided by the *Guardian* newspaper group which is the national newspaper with the largest selection of jobs. Accessible and impressive, this site is easy to search for jobs by relevance to your needs. It has many new jobs every day, listed by broad sector and seniority and includes a wealth of careers information including interview advice and tips.

This site is worth checking on a regular basis for national level jobs.

3. www.timesonline.co.uk
The website of *The Times* newspaper group. It contains their jobs pages, particularly useful for senior vacancies, managerial, technical and secretarial jobs. The site also includes topical interview tips and career development articles.

4. www.exec-appointments.com
This is the recruitment site provided by the *Financial Times* newspaper. It includes job vacancies, particularly in the financial sector and some job search tips.

5. www.jobs.co.uk
This site describes itself as a recruitment portal. It links up direct to all the sites it finds for you.

6. www.targetjobs.co.uk
This site covers graduate jobs and contains job seeking and interview advice.

7. www.reed.co.uk
This site is owned by Reed employment, a leading employment agency. It includes voluntary opportunities and career tips including interview techniques under the 'career tools' section. It labels itself 'the UK's biggest job site.'

8. www.bradleycvs.co.uk
A CV service company offering information about job search skills including interview techniques. This site also has many links to other specific recruitment sites.

9. www.monster.co.uk
A commercial recruitment website with extensive job search advice included.

10. www.workthing.com
A large commercial site with job adverts direct from employers, it also includes interview tips.

Index of questions

Education and training

Q1 Why did you decide to go to college?

Q2 Can you tell me about your college course?

Q3 Did you enjoy any particular part of your studies more than the rest?

Q4 Can you tell me about a project that you worked on at school or college?

Q5 Would you recommend your course to other people and, if so, why?

Q6 What do you feel you gained from going to college?

Employment history

Q7 Have you had any work experience?

Q8 Can you tell me about your last job?

Q9 What did you enjoy most in your last job?

Q10 What did you find most challenging in your last job?

Q11 Tell us about an area in your last job where you feel you could have performed better.

Q12 Why did you leave your last position?

Q13 What have you been doing since you left your last job?

Q14 What will your last employer say about you if we ask for a reference?

Q15 What would your colleagues from your last job say about you if we asked them?

Q16 What has been your greatest achievement in your working history?

Q17 Can you tell me about a problem that you have had to deal with?

Q18 What would you do if you had a problem that you could not deal with – perhaps if you were faced with a difficult customer?

Q19 Which of all your jobs have you found the most interesting, and why?

Q20 What are the most satisfying and the most frustrating aspects of your present/last job?

Interests

Q21 What hobbies or interests do you have?

Q22 Tell me about your favourite activity outside work.

General

Q23 What are your strengths?

Q24 What are your weaknesses?

Q25 What are you most proud of?

Q26 Which current affairs problem have you been aware of lately?

Q27 What do you see yourself doing in five years' time?

Q28 Why should we employ you rather than another candidate?

Q29 What other careers are you interested in?

Q30 Which other organisations have you applied to work for?

Q31 What does equal opportunities mean to you?

Q32 How would you put equal opportunities into practice?

Q33 When have you needed to be at your most tactful in your work?

Q34 What sort of person are you?

Q35 How would you describe your team/management style?

Q36 Are you a creative person?

Q37 What would you say has been your biggest mistake?

Q38 Have you made any career choices that you now regret?

The vacancy

Q39 Tell me what you know about this organisation.

Q40 Why do you want to work for this company?

Q41 If you were offered this job, how do you think you would spend your first two weeks with the company?

Q42 What do you think are the most important issues facing this organisation at the moment?

Q43 What do you think you can contribute to this company?

Q44 Why are you applying for the post?

Q45 Which areas of the job description are you weakest at and how would you compensate for this?

Q46 This job is too highly paid isn't it?

Q47 This job needs to be filled by a motivator – tell us how you would do that.

Q48 You will have some difficult characters in your new team. How will you handle them?

Q49 What do you think we should be doing to survive the economic downturn?

Q50 What do you think is the best way to deal with poor performers?

Index